Cosmic Laws

Author:

Sudabeh Moghadasi Bayat

Serial Number: P2146110067
Title: Cosmic Laws
Sub Tittle: Motivational
Author: SOUDABEH MOGHADASIBAYAT
ISBN: 9781989880685
Metadata: Self-help/Success/Mind, Body and Sprits
Cover Design: KPH Design
Book Size: A5/ 5.83 x 8.27 inches
Pages: 172
Canada Publish Date: January 2022
First Published Date: 2017
Publisher: Kidsocado Publishing House

All Rights Reserved, Including the right of production in Whole or in part in any form.

Kidsocado Publishing House
Vancouver, Canada

Phone : +1 (833) 633 8654
WhatsApp: +1 (236) 333 7248
Email: info@kidsocado.com
https://kidsocadopublishinghouse.com
https://kphclub.com

Dedicated to my dear parents, family, and all of the teachers who have helped me during these years.

Table of contents

Life 10

Love 10

Attraction of love 11

You are a magnet 14

Creation 17

Reality 22

Thanksgiving 23

Play roles 25

Karma law 28

How to achieve our goals? 31

The key to attraction 39

Positive thinking 45

Painting of dreams 46

What is belief? 47

Positive questions change your life 48

Feeling rich 49

Do not resist 52

Imagination 54

Victory	63
Faith	65
Creative mind	67
Emphatic phrases	73
Prayer	80
Frequency	84
Resistance	92
Leave out worries!	100
Why do I not achieve my goals?	102
Sign and inspiration	106
The law of belief	107
How are beliefs created?	109
How should we create positive beliefs?	110
Leverage of suffering and joy	112
Conscious and unconscious	115
Heart is the place of the divine message and the understanding of God's frequency.	116
Wealth	121
Trust	124
Health	128

The world is smart 131
Verses of blessing 135
Who is to blame for our miseries? 146
The law of evolution ....…..… 147
The law of attraction, vibration, and energy ... 148
Life-giving sentences ……….....…………… 152
You do not know how beautiful life is ……... 155
Law of abandonment ……………………..…… 156
What is your mission? ………………....…… 159
Self-confidence and self-esteem …………..….. 162
Belief in abundance ……………………….… 164
Last word ………………………………….....165

Preface

A majority of people spend many years of their lives finding a way to happiness and wealth or great relationships but never achieve their goals. After many years of trying, they have believed that either they have no chance or luck, they have been cursed, they must have money, or God does not want them to achieve their goals. I am here to tell you that all these beliefs are wrong. If I could, then all of you would and no matter where you live on this planet or what your family or religion is, you would achieve all your dreams. Believe that God wants you can achieve all your goals more than what you want. If you are dissatisfied with your current life, you must change your beliefs and attitudes. Let me fill your mind with the right beliefs. By reading this book, you will experience a good feeling and will realize how easy it is to achieve your goals. Achieving wealth and happiness is as easy as breathing. If you have a wish in your heart, believe that God has given you the power to achieve it.

Sudabeh Moghadasi Bayat

If you have started reading this book, you are probably looking for success, thus believe me that you will achieve it. Success can be acquired and you achieve it through study and experience. If you want to succeed, never stop reading books. You must read every day as you eat food. Book is the food of your soul. You do not have the opportunity to experience everything by yourself, thus learn from the biography of successful people. One of the secrets of successful people is to study and come up with great ideas. We have prepared a package for the first time in the world to provide you with biographies of successful people along with their books ... This package introduces the biographies of more than 200 successful people throughout the world. You can visit our website and prepare this unique package. Take time to read the biography of one of these people every day. However, the biographies of some of these people are long and you can read them within a few days. Getting successful seems logical for your mind gradually by reading the biographies of successful people and you realize that you are not different from the successful people in the world.

I promise you that your speed to achieve your goals will be multiplied. Keep it in mind that many
people enter this path but few of them remain and do not continue. Let me tell you an important point here; Persistence is the secret. Take a year and train your whole mind to succeed. Success comes after you. Use our books and tutorials. We show you not only the ways to succeed, but also provide tutorials for you to make money. Our website address is www.moghadasii.com. Please read every book several times to understand its points.
Golden tip: Between realism and optimism, please choose optimism to succeed.

Life

Your life is like this. There are positive and negative things in your life and you create them with your thoughts. In every field you think, health, money, relationships, job, or happiness. You are either healthy or sick. You are either rich or poor. You are either employed or unemployed. You either have a perfect relationship or you have a bad one. Your relationships are either good or complicated. Your job is either passionate and successful or unsatisfactory and frustrating. You are either full of joy or you are bored most of the time. You have either happy years or bad years. Good days or bad days. If there are more negatives than positives in your life, then there is a problem and you must re-examine your thoughts.

Love

There is only one power which is the power of love. Love is not just a feeling. Love is a positive force. Love is not weak. Love is a positive power in life. Love is the cause of all positive and good things. There are not hundreds of different positive forces throughout the world. Love is highly different from dependency. Dependency means that you are not happy without him and you consider your happiness in his presence; However, love means that both can be happy without each other and love each other. Please do not create a cage for your love. The great powers of nature such as gravity and magnetism are invisible to our senses while their power has been proven to everyone. In this regard, the power of love is invisible to us, but far greater than any power in nature. The power of love can be seen everywhere in the world. There is no life without love. Love is a force which makes everyone progress. Whatever you want to do or have comes from love. You have no progress without love; There is no positive force making you wake up in the morning, work, have fun, talk, learn, listen to music, or do anything at all. It is the positive force of love which motivates you to move and encourages you to do whatever you want, become whatever you want, or have anything. Love is the most powerful and at the same time it is very unknown in the world.

Attraction of love

What is the power of attraction? It means the power of love. When you feel that you are attracted to your favorite food, you feel love to that food. You will not feel this way without love. All kinds of food will be the same to you. You do not realize what you like or dislike because you are not attracted to anything. The law of attraction or the law of love ... they are both the same. Whatever you think of in your life, you receive in life. Based on the law of attraction, whatever you donate will come back to you. If you donate positive, you will receive positive. If your thoughts are negative, you will receive them negatively. Give positive to receive a life full of positives. If your thoughts are negative, you will have a life full of negatives… How do you provide things positively or negatively? Through your thoughts and feelings. Whatever you give, you will receive the same. Help someone whose car tire is flat in the street, of course, the same help will come to you very quickly

When you are angry at a family member who has annoyed you, the same anger will return to you somewhere in your life. Do you want to know who God loves and who He excludes from His love?

- Al-Anfal- 58: Surely Allah does not love the treacherous.

إِنَّ اللَّه لاَ يُحِبُّ الْخَائِنِينَ.

- Al Ḥajj- 38: Surely Allah does not love any one who is treacherous and ungrateful.

إِنَّ اللَّهَ لا يُحِبُّ كُلَّ خَوَّانٍ كَفُورٍ.

- Al-Qasas- 76:. Indeed, Allah does not like the exultant.

إِنَّ اللَّهَ لَا يُحِبُّ الْفَرِحِينَ

- An-Nisa- 107: Surely, Allah does not like anyone who is a sinful betrayer.

إِنَّ اللَّهَ لاَ يُحِبُّ مَنْ كَانَ خَوَّانًا أَثِيمًا

- Al-Baqarah- 190: God does not love those who overstep the limits

إِنَّ اللَّهَ لا يُحِبُّ الْمُعْتَدِينَ

- An-Nisa -36: God does not like arrogant, boastful people

إِنَّ اللَّهَ لاَ يُحِبُّ مَنْ كَانَ مُخْتَالًا فَخُورًا

Cosmic Laws

- Al-Qasas -77: Surely, Allah does not like the mischief-makers

إنَّ اللَّهَ لا يُحبُّ الْمُفْسِدِينَ

- Luqman-18: Allah does not like anyone who is arrogant, proud

ا نَّ اللَّهَ لا يُحبُّ كُلَّ مُخْتَالٍ فَخُورٍ

- Al-Baqarah -156: who, when a suffering visits them, say: "We certainly belong to Allah, and to Him we are bound to return"

الَّذِينَ إِذَا صَابَتْهُمْ مُصِيبَةٌ قَالُوا إِنَّا لِلَّهِ وَإِنَّا إِلَيْهِ رَاجِعُونَ

- Al Imran-134 : God loves those who do good

وَاللَّهُ يُحبُّ الْمُحْسِنِينَ

- Al-Baqarah-222: Surely Allah loves those who are most repenting, and loves those who keep themselves pure

انَّ اللَّهَ يُحبُّ التَّوَّابِينَ وَيُحبُّ الْمُتَطَهِّرِينَ

- Al Imran -134: God loves those who do good

وَاللَّهُ يُحبُّ الْمُحْسِنِينَ

- Al Imran- 146: Allah loves the patient

وَاللَّهُ يُحبُّ الصَّابِرِينَ

- Al Imran- 159: For Allah loves those who put their trust (in Him)

انَّ اللَّهَ يُحبُّ الْمُتَوَكِّلِينَ

- Al-Ma'idah-13: Allah loves the doers of good

إنَّ اللَّهَ يُحبُّ الْمُحْسِنِينَ

- At-Tawbah-4: Allah loves the righteous

إنَّ اللَّهَ يُحبُّ الْمُتَّقِينَ

- Al-Hujurat -9: Allah loves those who act justly

إنَّ اللَّهَ يُحبُّ الْمُقْسِطِينَ

You are a magnet

The world will bring everything back to your life based on whatever you think. According to the thoughts and feelings you send, you absorb wealth, health, communications, job, and every event and life experience like a magnet and you receive the same. When you send positive thoughts and feelings on money, you attract the positive situations, people, and events that bring more money to you. You attract negative situations, people, and events that cause the loss of money by sending negative thoughts and feelings about money.

Those who have a beautiful life talk more about what they love, and by doing so, they gain abundant access to all blessings of life. Talk just about what you love and love will release you! Nothing is impossible with the power of love. No matter what your situation is; The power of love can release you. Whatever you give to life, you will receive the same from life again. If you are positive, you will receive positivity but if you are negative, you will attract more negativity. No event happens accidentally in life. You receive everything based on what you send

There is no chance. Everything is based on order and this order is enforced by the law of attraction. No one receives injustice. Thoughts and words, have no power in life at all without feelings. You think about many things during the day which take you nowhere because most of the thoughts do not create any strong feeling in you. Do not worry because your thoughts, words, and actions are good ... Only having a good mood will guarantee that you are sending love and do not doubt that all this love will return to you! If most of the time you feel that you are neither good nor bad, you may think that you are in a positive mood, but in fact you are in a bad mood ... If you are in a

Cosmic Laws 15

really bad mood and then feel that you are neither good nor bad, such a mood reveals your bad mood.

Having a "neither good nor bad" mood is often a negative feeling because it is not a good feeling. Good mood means having good feeling! A good mood means you are happy, cheerful, eager, excited or passionate. When you think about money, your feelings reflect what you send about money. If you have a bad mood when you think about money, it is because you do not have enough money, thus you receive negative conditions and experiences indicating you have no money, as you have reflected such a negative feeling. When you think about your job, feelings tell you how you feel about your job. If you have a good mood about your job, you will certainly receive positive conditions and experiences because you reflect a positive feeling. When you think about family, health, or any other important issue, feelings let you know what your mood is. Life does not go on by chance. Life shows reaction to your thoughts. What you want is because of the good mood they give you. Now, how do you receive the good things you want in life? With good feelings! You have to send good feelings to bring good things to you. Money, wealth, and health are waiting for you to call them. There is no need to struggle and object to change your living conditions; All you need to do is reflect love through good feelings and everything you want will appear! Everything has a vibration and a magnetic frequency. Your feelings and thoughts have magnetic frequencies as well. Good feeling means that you are on the positive frequency of love. Bad feeling means you are on a negative frequency.

Frequency makes you attract people, events, and situations that are on the same frequency like a magnet. If you want to know about the secret of the universe, you must accept your thoughts based on energy, frequency, and vibration.

Every second is an opportunity to change your life as in most of the time you can change your mood. No matter what mood you had before; No matter how much you ruined your life, when you change the way you feel, you send a positive vibration and the law of attraction reacts instantly.

When you change your feeling, the past goes away and life begins to change. Try to change your vocabulary. Delete the negative words such as fear, hatred, awfulness, nonsense, and wrecked from your dictionary because when you say these words, they come back to you, which means that you consider nonsense flaws for yourself! Why do not you say beautiful words? Do you not think that using words such as wonderful, beautiful, interesting, amazing, and great are better? You might have experienced that sometimes you get lucky successively. There is only one reason that you have made love more than negativity in your life. You might have experienced the opposite that one tragedy goes after another when things go wrong.

These things happen because you have been more negative than positive and when you are more negative, more negativity comes to your life that attracts even more negatives. This is a highly important issue. If you do not pull yourself out of this defective chain, expect many bad things to happen. If you wake up in the morning and see that you are nervous and impatient, think about your thoughts a few days ago. You will realize that your thoughts have been constantly negative.

In order to make a difference in your life, all you need to do is to spend more time for being positive every day and enjoy life. For this purpose, you must think of positive

Cosmic Laws

things consciously because everything you see has both a negative and a positive aspect. It is up to you to choose which aspect to look at. Surely, those who look at the positive aspect of everything experience a more comfortable life.

Creation

First, you must be able to visualize what you want. Nobody can get anywhere without visualization. Remember to have your good feeling when visualizing. As you visualize, you must feel love for whatever you visualize. You must believe that you have achieved your goal and thank God for it. If you think about the non-achievement of your desire, you will feel shortage and a bad feeling. Golden tip: You must create the feeling of achieving your goal and be thankful before you get what you want. Keep it in mind that all your wishes exist in the world, you just have to put yourself in the orbit of your goals through gratitude. You must ask for whatever you want wholeheartedly. You will not have enough power to create your desire as long as you are not passionate about it. Your thoughts are like a boomerang which returns to you when you throw it away. Law of attraction is like a photocopier which does not make any mistake. You receive whatever you send. There is everything in the world. You just have to want it; Thus, when you imagine your dream house, it exists in the world. If it did not already exist, it would be impossible for us to think about it. When you vibrate through your own good feelings, your feelings create a magnetic field which completely surrounds you. Thus, this magnetic field is with you wherever you go. It is like a light which surrounds your body. A halo which surrounds each person is basically an electromagnetic field and you attract everything in life through the magnetic property of the field that surrounds you. Feelings determine whether your field is positive or negative at any minute! Do you want to believe that your wish is too big? But with this mentality, the vision will take you away from what you want. When you think that something is really big, you make the law of attraction understand that your wish is too big and difficult to achieve and it will probably take a long time; You are right because you receive whatever you think and feel. If you think that your desire is really big, you will achieve your wish very late while there is no big or small thing for the law of attraction and the law of time has no concept for this. It is our doubt which drives us away from what we want and often makes us lose the blessing we may have. If you notice that your faith is weak, talk to God to calm down. You must believe in God. Most people say we believe, but they prove the opposite in practice. They are impatient and sometimes blame God for their misery and say: God did not want us to achieve our goals. In fact, they blame God for their inability. They do not want to take responsibility for their lives. Feelings are inside you. This is the way to achieve whatever you want. Visualize whatever you want. Visualize the love and feeling of your goal ... Visualize every situation that you want and feel that you have it now. Spend 20 minutes every day to visualize what you want. Do it every day to get the feeling that you have already had whatever you want. Do it to be institutionalized on your mind. Fill your life with happiness. When you are happy, you feel great and you receive good things. A good mood brings everything you want in your life and if you take things seriously, life will deliver difficulty to you. You have power over life and you can design it as you want. Anyway, try to feel good. Fate

Cosmic Laws

is not by chance. It is about choice. This is your life. Clearly, every single experience of your life comes from every single thought and feeling you have sent. Believe it or not, your life is not by chance ... your fate is in your hands. Every thought and feeling determines the future of your life.

Life is like a menu; you just order. Choose whatever you like from that menu! When your dream car, your dream spouse, a fit body, children, and great characteristics are seen in someone, it means that you have the same frequency with such things! Be happy because it is happiness and excitement which chooses these things for you. Jealousy takes you away from whatever you want as jealousy is a negative feeling. In fact, you attract negativity and reject whatever you want with this great force of negativity. You create your own life. What do you think of yourself? Do you believe that you can do things but cannot do some other things? If someone tells you that you are less than someone else, do not listen. Such words weaken you and lower your self-confidence.

Do not listen to those who say you are not able to do such a thing. Tell them: Maybe you cannot but I can. You are a competent person. You are good enough right now. If you think you have done something wrong, start again. Forgive yourself. Let go of the past and take step on a new path. Do you believe that the world is what you see? Do the things you do not see exist? In fact, the same color you see in everything is not the same color. Everything absorbs all of the colors it has in itself and reflects the color it does not have in itself and you see that color; Thus, there is every color in the sky except blue. There are a lot of sounds you cannot hear as their frequency is higher than your hearing but they are real. You cannot see infrared and ultraviolet light since their frequency is greater than your vision ... If you visualize all of the known frequencies as the size of a mountain, all you can see is smaller than a tennis ball. You may believe that the real world is composed of visible and tangible three-dimensional objects but in fact nothing is three-dimensional; The car you are sitting in has a moving force including energy and space. Nevertheless, how real is the car? Notice that we, like God, are equipped with the power to create. He is the Creator of the universe and all of the particles of the universe are smart. We can announce our wish to the world but how is a wish created?

The Qur'an has mentioned the instantaneous creation of God and the power of inspiration and creation from nothing. As if everything happens quickly and time is completely meaningless. This is "Be, and it is" which applies to the whole universe.

- بَدِيعُ السَّماواتِ وَ الْأَرْضِ وَ إِذا قَضى أَمْراً فَإِنَّما يَقُولُ لَهُ كُنْ فَيَكُونُ

- the Originator of the heavens and the earth. When He decides on a matter, He just says to it, 'Be!' and it is.

  (Al-Baqara-117)

- قَالَتْ رَبِّ أَنَّى يَكُونُ لِى وَلَدٌ وَلَمْ يَمْسَسْنِى بَشَرٌ قَالَ كَذَلِكِ اللَّهُ يَخْلُقُ مَا يَشَاءُ إِذَا قَضَى أَمْرًا فَإِنَّمَا يَقُولُ لَهُ كُنْ فَيَكُونُ

- She said, 'My Lord, how shall I have a child seeing that no human has ever touched me?' He said, 'So it is that Allah creates whatever He wishes. When He decides on a matter He just says to it ''Be!'' and it is.

  (Al Imran-47)

- She said: "O my Lord, how shall I have a son while no human has ever touched me?" Said He: "That is how Allah creates what He wills. When He decides

Cosmic Laws

a matter, He simply says to it 'Be', and it comes to be.

- إِنَّ مَثَلَ عِيسَى عِنْدَ اللَّهِ كَمَثَلِ آدَمَ خَلَقَهُ مِنْ تُرَابٍ ثُمَّ قَالَ لَهُ كُنْ فَيَكُونُ

- الْحَقُّ مِنْ رَبِّكَ فَلَا تَكُنْ مِنَ الْمُمْتَرِينَ

(Al Imran-47-59 and 60)

Surely, in the sight of Allah, the similitude of the creation of Jesus is as the creation of Adam whom He created out of dust, and then said: 'Be', and he was

The Truth is from your Lord, so do not be of the constant wranglers.

- هُوَ الَّذِى يُحْيِى وَيُمِيتُ فَإِذَا قَضَى أَمْرًا فَإِنَّمَا يَقُولُ لَهُ كُنْ فَيَكُونُ

(Ghafir 68)

He is The (One) who gives life and makes to die; so when He decrees a Command, then surely He only says to it, "Be!" and it is.

- إِنَّمَا قَوْلُنَا لِشَىْءٍ إِذَا أَرَدْنَاهُ أَنْ نَقُولَ لَهُ كُنْ فَيَكُونُ

(An-Nahl- 40)

Surely Our only Saying to a thing when We have willed it, is that We say to it, "Be!" so it is.

- مَا كَانَ لِلَّهِ أَنْ يَتَّخِذَ مِنْ وَلَدٍ سُبْحَانَهُ إِذَا قَضَى أَمْرًا فَإِنَّمَا يَقُولُ لَهُ كُنْ فَيَكُونُ

(Maryam-35)

- It is not for Allah to have a son. Pure is He. When He decides a thing, He simply says to it, "Be" and it comes to be.

- إِنَّمَا أَمْرُهُ إِذَا أَرَادَ شَيْئًا أَنْ يَقُولَ لَهُ كُنْ فَيَكُونُ. فَسُبْحَانَ الَّذِى بِيَدِهِ مَلَكُوتُ كُلِّ شَىْءٍ وَإِلَيْهِ تُرْجَعُونَ

(Ya-Sin- 82-83)

Whenever He wills a thing, He just commands it "Be" and it is. So exalted is He in whose hand is the realm of all things, and to Him you will be returned.

Reality

There are other worlds and possibilities that you cannot see, but they exist. You must start a different reality! You must rebuild your life because whatever you say, good or bad, the law of attraction assures you that you have received it. The reality of everyone's life is different. You experience everything in your life that you believe in. For example, if you constantly say that there is no good girl or boy, the world will always put you in a situation where you see that there is no good girl and boy. Indeed, you see what you believe in. If you keep telling yourself that you are a victim of life, you will repeat it again and again. If you say that you are not as smart as other men, you are not as attractive as other people, or you are not as talented as others, you are right because the world shows you the same thing. Anthony Robbins has written a book called "Quantum Questions". In this book, he said: Change your questions to change your life. We have put it on the website for free. Download it and read or listen. One way of asking a question is to ask positive questions. Ask the questions which make you feel better when being answered. For example, what do I like? How much do I love good people? What else do I like? What can I see that really makes me happy? What can I see that excites me? What can I see that I wait for in my mind? What do I have to be thankful for? What do I like to hear? When you raise these questions, your mind has no choice but to answer them immediately.

As soon as your mind gets involved in answering your questions, it gives up other thoughts immediately. When you fail at controlling your mind, it can get out of the road like a car without brake. You are the driver of your mind; Thus, take control of it and keep it busy with your instructions on where to go ... If you do not tell your mind what to do, it will go anywhere it wants.

This mind is highly rebellious. Take control of it. The mind acts like an enemy to those who do not control it.

Thanksgiving

You cannot become rich without thanksgiving as it connects you to wealth. I know a lot of people who were in the worst situation and completely changed their lives by thanksgiving. I saw the things which were new to me. Every savior of the universe used thanksgiving because they were all aware that thanksgiving is the highest means of love and has a high vibration.

They knew that they could live in perfect harmony with the law of attraction if being thankful. Begin now and thank God for whatever you have. You can choose the person you love the most in this world and be thankful for having that person. Albert Einstein was one of the greatest scientists. His discoveries completely changed our attitudes to the universe. When Einstein was asked about historical developments, he only talked about thanking others. As one of the most intelligent geniuses of the age thanked for everything others had given him - a hundred times a day. It means that Einstein offered love at least a hundred times a day. Einstein obviously knew that thanksgiving had the highest degree of vibration. You will more of the same things if you thank God for the money you have, no matter how little because you will get more money. If you thank God for a relationship even if it is not so great, your relationship will get better every day.

When you thank God for your job even if it is not your dream job, you get a better job opportunity because thanksgiving is the most significant multiplier of life! If your only prayer in your whole life is thanking God, that is enough. There are lots of ways to use the power of gratitude in your life. Write them down every day and be thankful for them. Thank God for whatever you have received in your life. Thank God for whatever you receive in your life. Thank God for whatever you want in life, as if you have received them all. When you are thankful, it is impossible to feel sad or have any other negative feeling. Look for something to thank God if you are in a difficult situation. When you find something, look for the next and then the next thing since every single thing you find for thanksgiving changes your conditions. Thanksgiving is a bridge from the hell you have created for yourself to heaven. Thank God when something good happens to you every day. It does not matter how small it is. Thank God in any case. Thank God whenever you find a great parking spot, at the intersection when the light is green, and find an empty seat on the bus or train. These are all of the things you can be thankful for. Thank God for the immune system in your body that heals your body and for all of the organs in your body that keep you alive. Thank God for your extraordinary mind that no computer in the world can compete with. Your whole body is like a big laboratory that serves you for free every day. There is nothing the same in the world. Thank God for the trees, animals, oceans, birds, flowers, plants, blue sky, rain, stars, moon, and our beautiful planet. You should be thankful for every breath you take. Be thankful. Being thankful does not cost, but it is more precious than all the wealth in the world.

Being thankful pours wealth like rain on your life and enriches your life with blessings because whatever you thank God for, is multiplied!

Play roles

There is only one safe way to improve your mood for anything in life and that is creating and playing a game with the help of your imagination. Playing is fun; thus you really have a good mood when you play. If you watch TV movies carefully, you can see that some actors always play the role of the rich and some others always play the low-level roles. They act like that in their real lives. For example, imagine that Trump wants to play the role of a poor man. He cannot and his face does not look the poor. He has chosen the role of the rich in real life. Thus, the world does not give him the role of a poor man, because he has become rich mentally. If he loses his wealth, he will rise again. You are supposed to enjoy life. Play with the law of attraction. Play games with your imagination because the world does not notice that you are really playing or your actions are real. Whatever you give to your imagination and feelings, they will become real! How should you play? Just like actors. Do exactly what you do when you get very rich ... Logic takes you from point A to point B but it imagination takes you everywhere. Albert Einstein

For a person who believes, everything is possible. Jesus Christ

How do you feel about money? Most people say that they love money, but if they do not have enough money, they have no good feeling about it. If a person has as much money as he needs, he has certainly a good mood about it. The only difference between the rich and others is that the rich feel have much more good feeling about money. The reason why many people feel bad about money is that they have negative beliefs about money and such negative beliefs are rooted in their subconscious during the childhood. The beliefs such as we cannot afford. Money comes and goes! The rich are definitely fraudulent. Asking for money is wrong and is not a spiritual thing, having lots of money means working from morning till night, or having money does not cause humanity, etc. Most people receive such beliefs from their families. When you notice that there is no loss in any case, the whole world will belong to you. No matter what your financial situation is, no matter what the business, the country, and the world in which you live are. There is no such a thing as a bad situation. There were many people who lived in times of recession and their lives prospered since they were aware of the law of concentration and attention. They attracted whatever they wanted using this law by imagination and feeling and did not give up while facing difficult circumstances but rebuilt their lives. As you have a better feeling about money, you will attract more money. In order to change your mood, it is necessary to visualize your accounts full of money. You can imagine that they are not accounts at all, instead, you have decided to generously donate some money to the company or individual for the services they have provided to you. Imagine that accounts are the received checks and use thanksgiving law to thank the company that has sent you the invoice. For example, in case of electricity bills, thank the electricity department for their services. You can write on your bills; Thank you God for this bill. If you do not have money to pay the bill that moment, write "Thank you for the money" on the front. The world does not ask you if your image or feeling is real or not. It merely reacts to your action, that is all. If you have financial problems, you can send the thoughts on lots of money to the people who pass you in the street during the day to have a really good mood about money. Look at their faces and think that you are giving them a lot of money. Imagine their enthusiasm. Feel it and then go to someone else ... Doing so is very easy. If you really feel the mood, your feelings about money will change and your financial situation will change. You must do what you are interested in because working gives you enthusiasm. I mean you work as you love it! And when you love whatever you do, money comes after it! Stop complaining about your work and life; Do everything with love. Even when you do not know what your heart wants to do in life, you must send a good vibration through good feelings to attract whatever you want. The atmosphere of love will take you to your goal.

Golden tip: Success is not the key to happiness but happiness is the key to success. The biggest factor destroying a business boom is having bad feelings about failure. Even if your business is booming, you will create more recession in your business when you react with complaints.

All your hopes and wishes that make your business boom are on the frequency of love; Thus you must find the ways to feel good about your business and get to the highest possible frequency.

The world has unlimited ways to help you get what you want and money is just one of them. Do not be mistaken that money is the only way to get thing for receiving things. This thinking is limited and limits your life!

Cosmic Laws

Karma law

What a human plants, he will harvest; In other words, whatever human says or does will return to himself and whatever he gives, he will receive. If you see all the people as yourself, you do not hurt anyone because hurting them means hurting yourself. If you hate, you will harvest hatred and if you give love, you will receive love.
If you criticize, you will be criticized. If you lie, you will hear lie; If you cheat, you will be cheated. The subconscious mind has no sense of humor and people often cause unpleasant experiences for themselves with their jokes. What nonsense jokes we make together and are unaware that the world is not a joke. Whatever comes out of your mouth or any thought passes through your head, the same thing will return to you ... The abundance of blessings is always on the way of humans but it enters your life through wish and belief. Nothing but doubt and fear can cause a distance between human and his greatest ideals or intentions. As a person can make a wish without any fear, every wish of him will be fulfilled immediately. Jesus Christ says: O believers with low faith, why are you afraid? I know someone who always read the sign hanging on the wall of his room and suddenly he lost all his fears and his heart got filled with faith. The theme of the sign was: Why are we worried? It may never happen. These words were so institutionalized on his subconscious mind that now he believes that only goodness can enter his life. Therefore, nothing but goodness occurs. Telling good fortune in life is like this. If you tell good fortune for everything, you will complete it successfully. Pray in such a way as if you have received it. Pray with faith. You must act so that you have already received it. Every human owns what he sees and thinks in his dreams. Every great work and success occurs with not ignoring that picture on

Cosmic Laws

the mind; Usually before the great success, your frustration overwhelms you ... The one who is aware of the power of words is careful while speaking ... He should be careful of his words to know that what he says comes back to himself ... Humans constantly set rules for themselves with the words they say. If you keep talking behind other people's backs, you will bring all of them into your life. Horseshoe and snake nut have no power. It is the word and belief of humans that creates hope and expectation on the subconscious mind and brings good fortune. The only thing that can cause change on the subconscious mind is to emphasize that "there are no two powers. There is only one power: the power of God. Thus, there is no discouragement and it means courage. When you know that there is a God, you never anyone to give you job, money, or you do not beg your love to keep his/her relationship with you because you believe that everything is done by God's will. Talk to others about your dreams every day. Talk about the demand for healing, blessing, and happiness. Everything a person says about others, they will say about him and everything he wishes for others, he will receive for himself. Curse goes back to the person who says that. If a person wishes misery for someone else, misery will undoubtedly come to him. If he wants to help someone succeed, he has paved his way to success. Constant criticism causes rheumatism in the body as the thoughts coming from pessimism poison the blood and such toxins precipitate in the joints, your bones get painful, and life becomes unbearable. Basically, every disease is the result of a restless mind that constantly criticizes others instead of changing itself. Lack of forgiveness is the major cause of diseases, causes atherosclerosis or bone pain and also affects vision; If we want to say the names of these diseases, it will go to hell. Please forgive yourself for what you have done since God forgives all sins. Know God as very kind and merciful. Human's only enemies are within himself. Love your enemies, ask blessing for your cursers, do good things to those who hate you, and pray for those who have oppressed you. If you want to disarm your enemies, ask blessing for them. The Chinese say that water is the strongest element since it is completely non-resistant. Water can split a rock and take away whatever in front of it. God says that every good that comes to you is from me and every evil that comes to you is from you. Evil is just the product of human imagination. God is the absolute good. Repeat this phrase constantly: "I love myself and God loves me." I serve people and enjoy doing so. Ask blessing for your enemy to disarm him. In this way, you grab his ammunition and turn his arrows into blessings. This law applies to both individuals and nations. Ask blessing for all individuals of the nations to deprive them of the power of oppression. Cursing only enters your life. Repeat the sentence: "My work will go well today and I thank God for such a perfect day." Today, miracle comes after miracle and God makes me happy with his miracles. Whatever you wait for will occur. When human eliminates the image of poverty from the screen of his mind, he will become the ruler of wealth and his all wishes of will come true. Human takes back only what he gives. The game of life is the game of boomerangs; Human's thoughts, behavior, and words - sooner or later - return to him with a wonderful power. The person who trusts in God will never be forgotten and God is never late. Every day, ask God for your sustenance. Saving due to greed and hoarding has no end except poverty. Forgive whatever you do not need any more in order to receive more. You will not get much by selling extra items, but the doors of God's mercy will be opened to you by giving them. If human has complete faith in the source of his sustenance, he will own infinite blessings. However, faith or trust must be highly regarded in your life. Constant pretending affects the subconscious mind. If someone pretends to be rich and successful, he will become like that. Human has separated himself from his blessings by thinking of separation and poverty so much that sometimes he has to spend a lot of time on destroying his beliefs. Human must control his mind every second to see what he is thinking of. Control your mind to change your world. If someone humiliates money, they can never attract it. There are so many people in poverty by saying things as: I do not care about money or the rich are all thieves. God is the weariless provider of humans and His blessings are endless. Ask Him whatever you want without fear. The spiritual tendency to money is that the treasurer, with that greatness and glory, never fails! According to the ancients, a mother who does not care about her child is not a mother;

But now we know maternal fear is responsible for the bad things and events that happen to children because fear clearly depicts the disease or situation that the mother is afraid of. Good for the mother who can sincerely say that she entrusts her child to God and is sure that her child is under the protection of God.

How to achieve our goals?

They often ask me "how we should achieve our goals?" You must be only at the same vibration of your goal. Constantly ask for it with enthusiastically and ask God for guidance. Tell God, "Show me the way. Let me know if I have to do something." Pray every day. Prayer is your conversation with God. God, open the way for my sustenance; Let everything that is my right reach me right now in the form of abundant sustenance. God, I just hope in you. Forgiveness opens the way to receive. In order to have no financial problem, you must give of what you have been given. Even as a few bites of bread. Bills must be paid with joy and good feeling. Money should be given without fear but with good prayers with a happy heart. Doubt is a barrier in most of the ways. In order to overcome it, repeat this phrase many times: "I trust in God and seek refuge in Him from Satan." This word affects the subconscious mind and soon enough the person feels awake and conscious and takes the right steps with determination. Whenever human has hopes in God, he receives all his rights from this great treasury of blessings. Doubts, fears, hatreds, and regrets poison the human brain and make him sick. The only robber that robs all possessions of human is his own negative thoughts. Pray with faith as God has said: Call me, so I answer you. God will provide solutions for you. I have seen the people who have started a completely new job and have not encountered any problems without any prior preparation or with little training. Keep repeating: Everything I do, I take benefits because of God's kindness. Every human being has a compass called feelings within himself. You will not go astray if you walk with your feelings. Imagination is a creative power. You must always choose the words which are positive.

Human enters a world that God has provided sustenance and whatever he needs is already provided for him. However, he must open this treasury with his faith or with the words he says. Where there is fear, there is no good feeling. Feelings of security and happiness are the result of full faith in God. In other words, when human believes that an invincible power supports him and all his desires are met, he can feel satisfied and happy far from any stress.

Then, he will not get furious and sad soon. As he is sure that God protects his interests and he tries to enjoy life at every second.

If the person loses something, it indicates that there is a belief in loss on his subconscious mind. As soon as human wipes this false belief from his subconscious mind and says "whatever I have lost, God will give its equivalent to me." Accidents, aging, diseases, and failure are all the results of not giving up false mental perceptions. If human sees himself as God sees him, he turns into a transcendent being who is able to create because God has breathed His spirit into human. As said, whatever you hate comes to you; In other words, you attract whatever you have on your mind.

Human always harvests what he has planted in his world of thought. Spiritual tendency to money is that God supplies sustenance for human. Faithful human obtains any wealth and whatever he wants. Human aware of this fact loses his greed for money. He becomes fearless in spending and gives gifts to earn more from God. God brings His miracles in strange ways. You only attract the things which you think about infinitely. Thus, if you always think about poverty, you will attract poverty; If you always think about injustice, you will attract more injustice. Whenever we are aware that what we send returns to us, then we begin to fear our own boomerangs. Doubts and fears take you away from what you desire. You face a situation in which there is no hope. You will ask: What should we do now? Strengthen your self-confidence. Wherever there is no way, God opens a way! Your negative thoughts are your enemies: Live with positive thoughts. Feel yourself as rich and successful so that good feeling makes you rich. Nobody gives anything to you except yourself; And nobody withholds anything from you except yourself. " Game of Life " is a solo game. If you change yourself, all conditions will change. Change yourself to change the world around you strangely. Pray with faith and ask God whatever you want with good faith. When you pray, be sure that you have received it and it will be given to you. You believe that the God who owns everything will not let you carry a burden: even if it is a debt or anything else. Every time you feel the burden of life is heavy on you, leave it to God. Relying on your salary, income, savings, and capital can be lost overnight. But it is trust in God that makes you powerful. Relying on God provides sustenance. If you want to preserve your wealth, you must know that whatever you have is because of God; And what God gives you has no shortcomings and if a door closes, another door opens. People often say that they set aside money for the times of illness. They welcome diseases or we hear that people say, "We save for a rainy day. Undoubtedly, a rainy day will come in the most difficult conditions. Some believe that "We must expect worse conditions" or they say: "It will get even worse". Unaware of the fact that they welcome a worse thing by saying such words. But we see those who are always waiting for good news and positive change. Also, this group welcomes more favorable conditions. Change your beliefs to change your conditions. But how can you change your beliefs when you are used to waiting for poverty, shortage, and failure? Act as if you expect success, happiness, and abundance, begin every day with auspicious. People say: I do not go shopping because I have no money to buy anything. This is the reason why you have to enter the shops. You can put a banknote in your bag and go shopping. Buy whatever you want with your imagination. Your mind will gradually believe that you have money. When God is your hope, nothing is so

Cosmic Laws

strange to not happen. The things which are difficult for you are easy for God. Aladdin and the magic lamp means the objective image of the word. Aladdin stole the lamp and achieved all his wishes. Your thoughts are the magic light! Words and thoughts are a kind of radioactivity which bring you whatever you want ... A scientist has said that words are in a halo of light and human always receives the result of his words.

Prayer is your call to God and intuition is God's call to you. Relying on God needs a lot of power and courage. We often rely on God in small issues but we think it is better to do it ourselves when a big problem happens; In this regard, we prepare ourselves for defeat. People think that they can get rid of bad situations by escaping them while they are unaware that wherever they go, the situation is the same. Such experiences are repeated in their lives until they learn the lessons they should learn. The law of negligence says: Neglect anything you do not want and it will go out of your life. When you are no longer sad about anything, external worries will disappear. Whenever you realize the significance of every thought and word you say, you get used to being careful about your thoughts and words every day ... the way of abundance is a one-way street and has no way back. Recently, someone called me and said: I cannot find a job. Everything is stagnant.

I said: change your mind to find a job.

As Jesus Christ says: Do not complain about anything, but present your requests to God by praying and thanksgiving in everything. Praise opens the doors because hope and expectation always win.

Whenever someone asks me how I feel, I say: Gold is falling on me from the sky. Repeat this too to see its result. In order to gain wealth, you must have passion from head to toe. You must feel being rich. Be constantly ready for wealth. Become like a child and pretend to be rich because you affect the subconscious mind with hope and expectation. Intuition means the testimony of heart; In other words, as we say: I felt it! It does not mean to throw away everything you have but do not rely on them. Rely on your unseen treasury: i.e. the treasury of God. Practice positive thinking every day. Therefore, let us consider ourselves rich, healthy, and happy and see all our affairs full of divine order; But we must leave the way of fulfilling the wishes to the whole intellect. He has some tactics that you are unaware of; such tactics will surprise you. Repeat constantly: I am waiting for divine mercy. I am full of happiness. It does not matter what you do. Ask for guidance in any case. Seeking guidance lets you get rid of not only time and power but also misery. You have been negative in your whole life, but be positive from now. When human relies on the power of God - free from any constraints - he joins the absolute world. Let us understand this hidden power that we can understand wholeheartedly at any moment. Look with your inner feelings to achieve happiness. Leave false feelings. I have always asked you to repeat only the phrase that looks nice to your heart; I mean the word which gives you a sense of security and confidence. Speak about your work as little as possible only with those who inspire you as the world is full of those who have think negatively. The people who only say: it is impossible or you are very ambitious! God brings His miracles in mysterious ways. The problem of most people is that they want to know how and when they get whatever they want ... they want to tell God how to make their wishes come true. They do not rely on God's wisdom. When they begin praying, they set a task for to fulfill their demand. Thus, they put God in constraints and come with nothing but impatience. Leave your affairs to God and trust Him. Apparently, leaving affairs to God is easy in words but difficult in practice. How hard is it to trust God? Trusting God gives you an irresistible power because only God knows the way to do it. Trust him because He will do that. Many people use their own will instead of relying on God's power and always result in an unpleasant reaction. Personal will means we want to do things alone. Never try to change anyone. The only person who must change is yourself. When you change yourself, all the conditions around you will change too.

People will change too. Everyone's life is an objective image of the beliefs which are carved in their subconscious mind. Thus, you take the exact same conditions everywhere you go. God knows the way out and the way to fulfill every demand but we must trust Him.

Trust means trying to remain calm and getting out of His way. There are lots of those who are afraid of others or their unpleasant conditions. Of course, wherever they go, such conditions follow them. In this case, they must neglect the unpleasant conditions. Do not fight anything to drive it out because if it goes, it will bring back something similar. Thus, repeat this: I only want whatever God wants for me. I am at peace and relaxation. So, ask your wishes with praise to see the greatness of this law in the scene of action. Do not worry about anything but express your requests by praying and thanking God. Look at your past life to see how you brought happiness or misery into your life through your thoughts ... The subconscious mind has no sense of humor. People joke about themselves destructively while the subconscious mind takes it seriously. As you speak, you create a mental image that affects the subconscious mind and then such an image becomes external and objective. A person who is aware of the influence of the word pays high attention to his speech as it is sufficient to be careful of the reaction of his words to know that it returns to himself. The people who speak in anger or hatred make the biggest mistake as their words will have unpleasant consequences. Disgust and impatience steal power from humans. We must put these texts on the walls: Be careful of your thoughts. Be careful with your words! Whatever you pay attention to, you will become like it gradually. Thus, never talk about something destructive as you become like it over time ... Whatever you hate comes to you and whatever you are afraid of will be attracted to you. For instance, someone has mocked you and you are full of anger and hatred and you cannot forgive him. Time passes and someone else repeats the same thing to you again. The reason is that you have always thought about it and repeated it on your mind. So, it is repeated until you imagine what a useless person you are that everyone make fun of you. There is only one way to get rid of this situation. Ignore the injustice and forgive them all. You can easily get rid of this repeated subject. Always repeat the phrase: I forgive all my enemies and friends now and bless them ... Then, you will be surprised at how this law works. Bring order and harmony to your life by repeating that phrase. Do not look back and do not think about the hard times you had since you will be in the same conditions again. Give thanks for beginning a new day ... Seek refuge in God from anything that discourages you. Change your thoughts to change your world because your thoughts are your world. A woman once told me: I love to know about everyone's life. The joy of her life was gossiping. The sentences she used were: I was told that ..., I just realized that ... I heard that ..., Perhaps there is no need to say that she pays off for doing so because a great misfortune has come to her and all the people know about the details of her own life. Neglecting our own affairs and vain curiosity about others is a very dangerous thing to do. We must all focus on our own work. Nevertheless, we must be interested in the situation and mood of others with all kindness. The reason you have not achieved your goals yet is that you put your soul in a vibrating state that is not in harmony with the vibrations of your goals. In other words, you do not want your desire from the bottom of your heart. As a being who is the domain of immaterial energy, you can find the right thoughts. Achieve significant conclusions and decisions beyond what you have imagined. When you are in harmony with your dream, the extraordinary energy which created the world flows. In other words, passion, excitement, and victory are your certain destiny.

The better you feel, the better your relationship with God. If you feel bad, it means not having a relationship with God. Feeling good is equal to allowing the desire to be attracted while feeling bad is equal to not allowing the attraction and desire.

The key to attraction

In this human form, you are a creature made of flesh, skin, and blood. In addition, you are made of vibrations and everything you experience in your environment is through vibration and only through perception. It is with vibration that you can understand the material world. I mean you perceive and interpret the vibrations of whatever you see through your eyes. You interpret and hear the vibrations you receive using your ears. Even your nose, tongue, and fingertips convert vibrations into smell, taste, and touch while the most advanced vibratory interpreter in you is your feelings. Every thought has a vibration and every thought releases some signals and attracts similar signals.

This process is called the law of attraction. The key to attracting your dreams is for the vibrations of your being to harmonize with your dream and the easiest way to coordinate vibration is to imagine that you own it. Pretend that it is within your experience and focus your thoughts on enjoying that experience. By doing so, you allow that thing or experience to enter your life.

Thinking about things is like planning for the future and they are planning when you think of something on your mind. You are planning when you are concerned and worried. Worry creates something on your mind that you do not want. You cannot enter a bright room and hit the key to darken the room. In other words, there is no key to let the darkness enter the room and cover the light. In the absence of light, darkness comes by itself. In this way, evil comes automatically in the absence of good. However, resistance to health leads to sickness. In other words, when health goes away, something else comes along which is sickness. Just as a sculptor shapes a stone the same way he wants, you can convert energy the way you want. You shape energy through the power of concentrating constantly, thinking, remembering, and imagining events. When you speak, write, or listen, when you are quiet, when you remember, and when you think, you are focusing on energy and sending your thoughts out. Your dreams are sometimes radiated through talking and most often through the vibrations of your being. All of them are respected and answered. For instance, your car is old and needs to be repaired... its color is gone and you want a new car. This deep demand of yours causes the eruption of desire in you. The universe receives, accepts, and responds to it sincerely. In other words, if you constantly think of a beautiful car, the way to reach it will be paved but if you think about your old car in the middle of this thought, you will not achieve your goal. In today's advanced societies where you are immediately get aware of everything which happens in the world, thousands of thoughts run through your mind; Thus, it is impossible to control all of your thoughts. Instead, concentrate on whatever you have in your life. Achieving the desired feeling is more essential than guiding the thoughts. Having a good feeling, your mind will be in harmony with what is good for you. Based on the law, when you pay enough attention to something, the right vibrations will be found in you. The things you want or do not want will open the way to your life. It is impossible to control the conditions created by others. Some people try to build their happiness by dominating any event which may threaten their happiness, but unfortunately, as they put more pressure on unwanted things, they get coordinated with them more and enter them into their lives. As a result, they become more convinced of how destructive the threatening thoughts were. Instead, insist on your beliefs and try not to dominate the thoughts of others or other events to let the world help you and fulfill your dreams.

When you cannot think positively and are not focused yet, the initial vibrations are insignificant and have no power of attraction. Thus, you do not see any sign of the emergence of desire in these early stages; But your mind attracts the thoughts which are in harmony with it and becomes stronger, its attraction power increases, and other thoughts which have the same vibration join it and this thought creates a good feeling in you and its sign is that you are in harmony with the energy of your origin; If you do not have a good feeling, it shows that it is not in harmony with your true being. Most people are not the creators of their thoughts, but their thoughts are a function of what is happening around them. They observe and find an emotional feeling in reaction to what they have seen and as they have no control over what they have seen, they conclude that they have no control on their intellectual and emotional reactions. We want to inform you know that you have full control over your emotional fixation and you can change it and give it more power and capacity. The feeling of passion shows that you have a strong desire. In addition, feelings of anger or revenge are the signs of intense desire while the feeling of sadness indicates little desire in you.

Your feelings are the absolute indicator of the vibration in you; So, they show how your ability of attraction is. They determine whether or not you allow your wishes to be fulfilled at any given time. Changing the vibration pattern is not difficult, especially if you know that it can do it gradually. Therefore, here is a question for you: how can I harmonize myself with the vibration of my dreams and the answer is simple: pay attention to your feelings and select your thoughts consciously no matter what, just be something that you want and when you think about it, it must create a good feeling in you. You approach your desires with a feeling of happiness. In the process of moving towards your dreams, you will always feel happy. There is a lot of comfort and convenience, thus you should not be worried about the risks to move towards it. You must know that it takes time for your thoughts to come to result, thus you must give yourself plenty of time to assess, decide, and enjoy the creation process. The only reason for you to achieve something other than what you want is to focus most of your attention on something else - without knowing it. You achieve whatever you think of, whether you like it or not. After practicing for a while, you will realize that the laws of the world are fixed, do not tell lie to you, and do not change. Such laws do not confuse you.

Cosmic Laws 43

The world responds carefully to the vibrations you provide. When you get aware of the power to guide your feelings, you know how significant your current thoughts are and you realize that you will be relieved and enjoy your journey with patience when you find this awareness. For instance, you want to cook and there are things in this kitchen which are not appropriate for your work. There is no need to use them. On the other hand, you are not sad about being in the kitchen. You just use the right ingredients to cook your favorite food and put away the rest of the ingredients. The diversity of whatever in the world should not frighten you, on the contrary it should inspire you because you know that each one of you is not the creator of a separate experience. Have you ever heard of the radars in seafaring and aviation that exist in ships and aircrafts? The positioning system never asks "Where have you been?" Or "Why did you stay there all this time?" Its mission is to take you to the destination through the shortest route. Your feelings provide you with the same guidance system because their task is to get you from where you are to where you want to be. The greatest gift you can give others is your happiness. When you are happy and joyful, you are fully connected to the pure stream of positive energy of the origin and your reality. When you are connected, everything and everyone you care about takes advantage from such attention. Your happiness does not depend on the behavior of others but is related to your inner vibrations. In land journeys, you are not worried about the route because you know the distance between the two cities. You know where you will pass during the journey and you know what will happen if you go in the wrong direction. You will never be wrong with what you want to be when you get aware of your emotional guidance system. In addition, you know that you are closer or farther from your goal with every thought you present. The only way is to stop thinking or paying attention to what you do not want at all. Thus, when you do not pay attention, it will not become part of your existence. Any conditions, even very difficult, will change by changing attitudes and thoughts. Biting thoughts needs a lot of practice and concentration. If you focus on what you are now and think as always and your ideas are as always, nothing will change in your life. Nobody knows what is best for you except yourself. At any minute, you know what is best for you. When you become aware of the power of your thoughts and the power of accepting the things you want, you take control of life and its events. Love and self-praise is an aspect that you can develop in yourself. Self-praise is in full harmony with the vibrations of the source energy. Thus, when you believe that your dreams will come true, you are in a creative situation but when you want something that you do not believe in, it will never happen to you.

Vibrations become activated within 17 seconds of focusing on something and as the concentration is stronger, the world will bring newer thoughts to your mind, being in line with your original thought. If you can concentrate particularly on a subject for 68 seconds, the vibrations will become so strong that begin to manifest. When you are aware of your emotional state, you can guide your thoughts in a way to only attract the desirable and pleasant things. When you do not have a good feeling, you should correct your feelings so that you are not attracted to something unwanted. Voluntary creation does not mean changing the conditions and then spirit. Voluntary creation means selecting the thoughts which will change your mood and this change of mood, emotions, and feelings will attract dreams.

Positive thinking

Look around and find something that makes you feel good. Try to focus on this thing and think how beautiful, useful, or amazing it is and continue focusing to increase your positive thoughts. This method creates strong vibrations in you. Try to find the things which are certainly praiseworthy because the goal is not finding imperfect and bad things. The more you focus on good things, the more the law of attraction provides you more with good thoughts, people's experiences, and things which are in harmony with your good mood. The more you define everything positively, the less resistance will be found in your existential vibrations. The less resistant you are, the better your life will be. You can transfer yourself to higher vibrations and avoid the negative thinking mood by practicing the process of praise. After a while, you will experience a feeling of constant vitality. Your acceptance power will increase after a while due to practice. At the beginning, it is good to practice this for 10-15 minutes every day. After a few days, you will see that you are doing this several times per day, even if you do it here for a few seconds and there for a few seconds. Nevertheless, it gives you the same good feeling.

When you are always giving thanks, complimenting, and praising, you are connected to the center of energy and you rely on it. Thus, you are no longer vulnerable, you are not scared, and events do not worry you.

Painting of dreams

First, the painting of the things you want should be so beautiful to make you happy every time you look at it. Write On the wall where your eyes can easily see: Everything I want is there.

The more you think, pay attention, and not resist, there is no doubt that you will achieve all this and your inner feeling will become better. The doors open to you and you simply achieve such desires. Your world is in this painting. You are just like the lamp genie sitting on a chair that can go anywhere in the world and obtain whatever you want; So, you make a wish for having a beautiful house and you build it in the city you love, you provide income for yourself, prepare whatever you want. You provide all beautiful and lovely things you want and put on this painting. You can just play this game mentally, but if you really prepare a painting and put the things which reflect your dreams, you will enjoy it more. Focus on each of these dreams and write down why you want each of them. The thinking step focuses on your instant and important life experiences. When you think why you want these things, your inner resistance reduces and your thoughts become clearer; But do not forget you achieve your dreams if you ask how, when, and how. Your inner resistance will increase, especially if you have no answers to these questions. This list becomes more developed by addressing each detail and writing a list on the details. If this list gets longer, it will increase more energy in you and you will reach your goal sooner.

Remember that whatever we offer takes a little time from you every day and health, vitality, wealth, and good relationships and everything necessary for a full life will be attracted to you. When you play your future life with the happiness, not only your financial situation but also

Cosmic Laws

other aspects of your life will improve. This game will not only increase the vibrations around the things you want, but also attract your favorite things to you.

What is belief?

Any thought which is repeated on your mind is called belief. Some of your beliefs are highly useful: the thoughts which are in line with your knowledge of the origin and thoughts which are in line with your desires ...; But some beliefs are not good such as the thoughts which indicate your unworthiness and incompetency. We tell our friends in this world that the reason we recommend meditation is to clear your mind very simply and quickly. It is only enough to open the door. All this flows to you and then you have to think for all this joy! You feel good when you focus on whatever your heart wants. If you focus on the lack of what you do not want, you will have a bad feeling. Pretend that your pencil, pen, or paper is magical and whatever you write comes true.

By doing so, you will do two essential ways to achieve your dreams. Firstly, you will focus on what you want, and secondly, you will eliminate resistant thoughts. The main character of this text is you. The others play the next roles. Determine who plays in this play and then write the initial plan. Writing a plan is highly important and the goal is to feel the life you want to have. If you re-read this text repeatedly, it will become a strong image on your mind. The powerful image has energy vibrations and such vibrations make the images come true. Take the paper and draw a line at the top of the page and write on the right side:

"The things I have to do today" and then write in front of it "the things I want God to do for me". Now, look at the long list of things you must do today and select the things you really want to do. In the section "The things I have to do today", enter the things you have to do today and then write the rest of your work under the heading "the things I want God to do for me".

You are a receptive being and the thinking process happens to you quickly. You should be able to focus clearly on whatever you think and want, but this focus is impossible due to the mental confusion caused by multiple thoughts. Let me give you an example. They tie the legs of baby elephants to a nail driven into the ground with a 2-meter rope. At first, the baby elephant tries hard to tear the rope but it fails. After a few days, it gets tired and stops trying. After a few years, when it becomes a multi-ton elephant, they tie the same 2-meter rope to its leg.

But it no longer tries to tear the rope. Do you know why? Because it believed it could not tear the rope. The elephant believed that it does not have the power and cannot do anything. It believed that it could move up to two meters and its range of motion was the same. The effect of our mentality, attitude, belief, or perception of the world is so great that we may be trapped in the shackles of the mind like an elephant forever. Such a mental captivity does not let us change and achieve new progress and balance. Look what beliefs do to us. Beliefs are so powerful that they can paralyze human to stop trying.

Positive questions change your life

Those who always say why do I suffer from so much misery? do not know what trouble they make with their lives because the mind has to look for an answer to your question and so finds the answers to show you why you are miserable. When you say, "What if I achieved this desire?" another type of expectation is aroused in you that is less resistant. This question will arise a positive reaction in you so it will get you more easily to whatever you want or what if we spend more time with our friends? What if the roads are vacant and we reach our destination more easily? What if we have a good day at work? What if I find a good partner for my life? The reason why this phrase is important is that the type of phrase is soft and easy and causes less resistance. If you want to know how you feel about a subject, you can describe everything. More importantly, you have to express your feelings.

Feeling rich

First, take a 50000-toman bill or less and put it in your bag or pocket. Always carry it with you and keep it in mind that the money is there. Always feel satisfied that it is there and think about the feeling of security it gives you. Now, think about the things you can buy during the day with this bill. When you walk past a fancy restaurant, tell yourself that if you want, you can go in and order a delicious meal. When you walk past a clothing store, keep it in mind that you can buy a beautiful blouse or pants if you want. By keeping this bill and not spending it, you will receive the vibrations whenever you remember. If you do not spend this money and use it only on your mind, its vibrations will reach you 20 -30 times and it will be as a you have spent a thousand tomans easily for your own heart. Having negative feelings is like an alarm that informs you know that you are attracting bad things. An easy solution is to wait until you feel bad and tell yourself what I want is having food feelings. Laugh more, cry less, have more optimistic predictions and less bad predictions. Nothing is more significant than having good feeling. Practice it and see what happens. We tell you that you really have that power that always works for you, just ask the world to do something for you. Can you believe that if we say that you can stay in this world as long as you want, provided that you have a lively life and attract your desires without resistance and negative thoughts, your desires and aspirations will make the force of permanent life flow towards you and you will continue your life with enthusiasm and joy. The person who has dreams is the one who loves living and the person who does not have any desire does not want to stay in this world. Take the life easy. You are used to taking life seriously and working hard. Life is a play which should not be taken too seriously because your life is limited on this planet. Accept new and fundamental thoughts about yourself. When you were born in your mother's womb, you became under the control of cultural conditions to live with a normal standard of living, in fact you accepted what life has offered to you. You are often planned in such a way to believe that you do not have the understanding or ability to make your dreams come true. In fact, there is an awareness that you can live there voluntarily, where you can change your perception of yourself as a being and find yourself satisfied with all the dreams you have. Habit means that everything you do is planned for you by your culture and family. In other words, you adapt yourself to everything. You study hard, follow the do's and don'ts, complete the work and employment forms, pay your taxes, find a job, and do whatever the citizens of a community do. Then you retire, have grandchildren, play with your

Cosmic Laws

grandchildren, and finally die. In fact, I want to emphasize that there is nothing wrong in this scenario, everything is excellent, and if such a model in life is acceptable to you, then you no longer need to read this book. The ideal of your soul is what you want and have more than anything. The ideal of your soul is greatness, space and expansion, and one of the things it needs mostly is that it wants to be expanded freely. This is the new concept of yourself, something that comes from your soul. The constituents include everything you accept as the truth about what your body's external physics. Everything you believe as your innate abilities and everything you have learned in life is an external concept of yourself. The external concept of yourself includes your attitude to your health, security, and susceptibility to disease. You know that if you are prone to being overweight or addicted to different substances such as sugar, caffeine, fat, meat, dairy, and things like that, it is you who sets the boundaries for receiving and acquiring such substances. The inner concept of yourself is the beliefs about it and the intelligence that constitutes the major part of your being. I often consider the inner world as a soul in a machine human. If you desire to be a person who has the ability to realize all his dreams in life, you need to move to a higher level of yourself and intervene in the events of your life. It means that you have to cope with difficult things, which is often considered as a change in your concept. Remember that concept is what you believe to be applied to the inside and outside of you. Currently, the beliefs which have built in your life can be called to be right or wrong

Do not resist

What I encourage you to do is that if you want to be happy and relaxed, you must overcome the inner resistance that all you have is the earthly life. Unique people have a burning desire to succeed while this burning desire for a dream is different from achieving a normal success. When this desire burns the human, it does not come from inside the human. Having an inner awareness along with a burning desire is one of the basic requirements to become a person who can express his desires and wishes. Nobody can say where thoughts come from and how they are formed. However, we have generally accepted that we think and try to make all our thoughts come true, I have had such a view for most parts of my life. Open the windows of your mind to new ideas and ways of thinking. This will help you change your mental concept. You can even consider yourself as a divine and infinite being instead of trying to consider yourself as a human being who has no choice in choosing the thoughts which come to his mind. This new way of living makes you understand what I mean by the highest personal concept of yourself. Have an open attitude to the experience of things which used to limit you in any way. Remember this sentence: You have no limits to what you want to do. The part of you that you believe in is defined by what you have achieved, won, or owned. This is a belief that proves that you are a creature with your own specific abilities and limitations. You may be surprised if you know that there are beliefs which can put you on the path to happiness, success, health, and whatever you want. The idea of having a higher self is always higher than the concept of the self, that is normally defined globally as ego. In fact, the higher self contains higher and superior characteristics than me. Quantum physics states that ego is in your

Cosmic Laws

possession. The time you are reading a paragraph differs from the time you are reading a previous paragraph. This is the nature of the physical world that keeps us all alive. What is real? A spiritual body responds immediately: something is real that never changes and your body is not real as long as it is constantly changing. The Creator has left a piece of Himself and a spirit of His nature in every creature by which a creature can be a creator; It means that you can work with your mind, power, and spirit to get the elements you need instead of waiting for your needs to be met by an external source. This is a great image for you to begin understanding your superior soul. There is a light from God inside you that is not personal and you cannot receive it by feeling

That light makes the heart to beat, hair to grow, and your lungs to exhale. As the light of God increases, you must say: The part of me that belongs to God is complete. Jesus Christ said: " Everything is possible with God. »

Use this positive phrase several times. I am powerful. God is the greatest source of love. The highest position in love belongs to God and He always remains in this position. You have this feeling of pure love in your soul. There are things in the world that human cannot do, but God can do all of these things. Now, everything is possible. Do not delete anything. Your respect increases when you are close to God and you are close to God when you feel being needless in your life. God is the closest one to you. You cannot get close to God unless you try to be with God. When you know this great claim, you will receive your source power as if you get disappointed of your source, you will not have a long life. You see God who is unique in His form and you are one of those superior forms. Whatever you connect with is a series of messages from the world of love, peace, and pleasure. In fact, we have infinite power to achieve our fulfilled dreams which are one with the source of our existence. That is why I showed "I am" and inspired you to explore its content. "I am" is a full activity from God, and each of us can unite so that our "I am" is a reflection of the God we are. The word "I" is united with your divine spirit and reminds you that you are divine and have the same power of creation as God. Note how your family members or close friends use the inherent power of "I" in their lives. Many people say I am weak, poor, greedy, upset, cowardly, and ignorant, and attempt to bring these issues into their working lives.

If you want to listen to them and then change them, you will gently remind them that they do not have to attract such negative thoughts and accept them as their inner reality. Do not argue, just gently notify them. You can become one with your "best soul" by observing and being aware of me.

Imagination

Imagination is more significant than knowledge. Knowledge is always limited while imagination surrounds the world. God's greatest gift to you is giving imagination to you. There is a capacity for your realized dreams inside of you. There is the greatest power you can imagine in your imagination. It is in this realm that you can rule your world with your inner powers arbitrarily. You can imagine whatever you want and accept that it is for you. Have no doubts. Do not have any discomfort, rush, or fear. All knowledge is with you. Look around. Everything you can experience with feelings was once imagined by others. This is a big fact that you must understand. There are many phenomena which have been once fantasy before entering this world. It must first come in your imagination. The process of creation and invention stops without imagination. You have this great power in you that is truly unlimited and has been given to you as your right. Today, the world of quantum physics emphasizes that the universe is made of supernatural energy and particles are not composed of any particles. Everything is originated from something else is the same in your imagination. You cannot touch, taste, hear, or smell it. There are no boundaries. You cannot prove the world with mathematical formulas or scientific research. All of us know that it exists. These thoughts of you are the beliefs which penetrate you. The imaginary ideas which are always in you have not been proven in scientific fields. Perhaps the most common misuse of imagination is the emphasis on not wanting something for yourself. This kind of using imagination is the biggest mistake.

Pay attention to general conversations and you will understand its unbelievable nature. Imagine finding these phrases: I do not deserve this success, I am miserable, nothing helps me, I am not healthy, and I cannot get better. These are the beliefs which may have been remained in our minds since childhood. People with such beliefs have not been able to imagine high performance of their true selves and realize their dreams. Begin paying attention and letting go of your imagination. Instead of imitating, practice to fill your creativity which is full of beliefs and dreams that you want to maintain. Respect your imagination, regardless of whether others think it is ridiculous or impossible. Believe in whatever in your imagination and what has not entered the physical level yet. Never enter anything you do not want into your imagination. Never let your imagination be pessimistic about your negative beliefs about life. Use your imagination to know God and realize your dreams, leading you to a higher awareness of yourself. Believe that your imagination is only for you. In fact, it is the boundless area of your mind which no one has access to. Nobody can enter your imagination and enter the things they prefer. In addition, no belief can enter your glorious imagination and pull you out of your beliefs. Your imagination is a fertile ground for every seed to grow. This law recommends you to never let anyone enter your imagination to say what is possible or impossible for you, how to think, who you should be, or any other opinion. Note that some of these ideas may have been really recommended by the goodwill of others and take you back to your childhood. Never believe in the beliefs of someone who can ruin your dreams or imagination. This is your property. Place the no-entry sign on your imagination. Do not let your imagination be limited by the normal circumstances of your life. Your imagination is unlimited and if you select it for the ordinary level, you will stay at the normal level of your life with your old thoughts with the idea that everything that exists now is the reality of life. Such a guide will help you whenever you have no experience with the purpose of life or when you prefer to enter negative feelings such as fear, anger, hatred, enmity, and unhappiness into your life. Each of these feelings takes you away from God. Be as happy as you can and enjoy life. Why are you scared of God? God is love and unique. If you are scared of God and are upset or angry, how can you love others? Fear, sadness, and hatred hurt your heart. God is very kind. Rely on God's kindness so that your heart is filled with joy. Be careful how you play with words.

Cosmic Laws

How do you use the words which have a bad meaning? Saying beautiful words transforms your life. Practice using your imagination to define yourself only in a positive way with beautiful thoughts. Do not place any restrictions on your imagination and save the analyzed beliefs in a private place so that nobody can discourage it. Put a "no-entry" sign on your imagination to remind you of a private path. My life is a picture of my imagination in reality. I live like this and nobody can take me away from this way of life as I do not intend to go anywhere else. I just know that if the whole world distracts me from stupid dreams, nobody can take my imagination from me. This is a mental base that you can choose. Your imagination can be turned into material reality when God knows, so forget how to do it and live in your imagination. This is a great power that you have if you want to accept it as your own. I emphasize how vital it is for you to claim this inherent power of God in you and you can use it for life. Be persistent for having access to this idea. Stick to your dreams constantly and live as if the belief you have in your imagination is your nature. We are energy in the first place and our physical body is the result of expressing our energy. If we change our energy, we can change our physical reality as well. God has no physical body and is only energy. In addition, this divine energy is not like the energy of the material world that your senses have reported. When you realize your glory, you are attracted only by the glory of your life and if you believe in "love", you will attract love. The best way to attract the best things is to love yourself. This love attracts the things in your life that you can hardly believe and this is a simple fact.

If you say "I am weak" you have dishonored the name of God in you. How is weakness possible for this source of creation - the source of energy responsible for the creation of the world? This is not written in your law. How can you live with your superiority while thinking "I am weak"? Are you authorized to define yourself in such a blasphemous way?

By thinking "I am strong", you put the things in your imagination that you needed and you became united with the source of "being strong" instead of "being weak". Instead of saying "I cannot find my desirable job," say, "I can." Do not say "I cannot live in peace" but say "I am in peace." Do not say "I am not lucky in love", but say "I am lucky in love". Say "I am happy" instead of saying "I am not happy." The phrase "I am" that you always use for describing yourself is a sacred phrase for the name of God. Consider the highest dimension of yourself.

Leave out your usual habits and do not use contemptuous terms to describe yourself. One of the great lessons of the phrase "I am" is that it immerses you in the thought of your divine self. In fact, praising God allows you to progress.

Everything is possible with God. Your imagination is yours. You are free to put anything in your imagination: "I am talented, heroic, happy." Do not be scared of the sentences like "I am valuable and satisfied" and let life be your reality.

Your conscious mind is a hidden and personal factor. This dimension of your being is the factor of making decisions and choices and is always aware of what you do and how decisions affect your voluntary activities. Thoughts are replaced by "feelings" in the subconscious mind. No thought is carved on the mind unless it is felt, but when it is felt, you must accept its consequences. Good feelings determine good things and bad feelings determine bad things. "Feeling" is the only intermediary through which thoughts are transferred to the subconscious mind. Begin to feel the thought that you have placed in your imagination. Remember that this is the same feeling that happens in your body when you think about whatever you like or the goal you want to achieve. Close your eyes and experience those feelings in your body. Your imagination can realize all your desires to the extent of your attention. Your inner treasure will divert you from living in a world of unlimited abundance. Always live with the inner feelings of "I am happy, I am rich, I am perfect." You can program your subconscious mind with the help of your imagination to create some experiences which match your inner feelings. Your subconscious mind controls about 96% of what you do in your life as if you are on an automatic guide to everything you do in your life. The last 20 minutes of the day, before you fall asleep, are the most critical minutes of your day if you want to start a life with fulfilled dreams. In this short part of your day, you must tell your subconscious mind how you are feeling and what God is going to fulfill when you wake up. This 20-minute part in bed that you enter the subconscious mind and fall asleep about 10 hours later, is the most vital part of your day. This 20 minutes before bed is the last power of your heart for your subconscious mind. You must focus on making the wish you have imagined to come true.

The feeling that comes from answering the question, "How will I feel if I achieve all my dreams?" is the same feeling that should occupy all your attention before going to sleep.

Before sleeping, you must be aware of what you want to be or like to have. Keep this magic phrase in mind: You are taken from God. That invisible part of your being is in fact a mind belonging to God as long as you do not forget God. If your subconscious mind receives the belief in being rich, you will become rich. If your subconscious mind receives the belief that "I am happy," "I am in love,"

"I am intelligent," or any phrase you make with faith, it will make it your material reality.

Before going to bed, you must prepare yourself as if you are going to a holy place ... Never go to bed with negative thoughts in your head because it will create a great damage to your subconscious mind. If you think of failure, you will attract deprivation. If you think or say that I can do nothing, I am stuck, my life is out of control, the power of such thoughts becomes the opposite of the power of the dream life. Thus, it resists to the realization of the dreamy life.

Remember that thinking about failure leads to more deprivation, and if you continue to think like this, the universe will send you a force which the heavy scales will stick to the ground and you will stay in the same position. You can direct your thoughts with positive thoughts, i.e. thinking of a happy life so that it is in line with your dreams and let the world provide you with new opportunities. Note this the world is limited but the world of the mind has no boundaries and grows from planting the seeds of your great dreams. You will obtain whatever you think of. Thus, it is better to think about your dreams and pay no attention to their difficulty or impossibility. Put the power of your dreams in your mind and think along with it to attract sufficient energy. Do not forget that the price of buying this force is your only thoughts. Thus, do not spend it to buy whatever you do not need. Mitigate useless struggle with skill and conscious effort. For this purpose, you need to calm your brain. Spend more time enjoying life and looking at stars, clouds, rivers, storms, creatures, and nature thoughtfully. Then, spread the same kindness due to relief to others. First, begin with the family. Spend more time on playing loudly with the children, listening to them, and sometimes reading them stories. Go on an excursion with someone you love and tell them that you love them wholeheartedly. Do the same at work, in society, and even with strangers. Try to give your place to someone else in the queue instead of being in a rush. When you reach a yellow light while driving, stop and avoid driving like crazy instead of speeding up and do not think about getting there two minutes earlier. Give way to drivers in the crowded streets even if you are right. All of these are the ways to begin to change direction. Create peace and enjoy life. If people escape from you, know that the vibration of your thoughts is scary and upsetting, and in simple terms, you have no balance. In order to be aware of your effect on others, make a list of those who are honest with you. Then, ask them how they see you so that you can understand what others think of you and compare it to your self-perception. You have never done anything wrong. You have not failed - you have only had the behaviors which had some results. The question is not why you behaved wrongly, but the main question is what do you do with such results? If you choose shame and guilt, you will become weak more than any other feeling and withdraw from life. Sometimes, you will not want to be alive anymore. The better way is as follows: You have no flaws in life right now in whatever conditions you are in. You had to endure this trauma and disappoint others with your abuse. You had to fall to the point where you know where the problem comes from and you need adjustment and reach yourself to superiority with the power of thought and realize that you are still a divine being and all of the weaknesses you feel in yourself is not in harmony with love for God. Ask God for guidance and pray for an exciting force, power, health, and peace in your heart in a state of despair. If you are not feeling well, return to this path of peace immediately, forgive yourself, and immerse yourself in the love of God so that your life becomes adjusted once again. If you attribute despair and unfulfilled needs to God, you always have an excuse to accept whatever happens; But God is extremely eager to bestow abundant blessings on human beings. In fact, God is an absolute blessing, but human goes out of the way of happiness by himself. If you consider the shortcomings as the will of God, you will create a great resistance to the blessing and the universe will send you more and more of what you believe. If something bad happens to you, you are not miserable, but your mind and that bad event had the same vibrations at that moment. If you think in this way, you can adjust the world to the vibration of your mind and become harmonized with what you like. By changing low vibrations into high vibrations, you move the energy that is in line with your great desire. I want you to focus your thinking on being vibrant and put aside the attitude of happiness versus misery. In fact, your thoughts are your property and when they move towards a certain goal with perseverance, they will be turned into wealth or whatever you want. When someone is ready to work, he shows himself at a short time. One of the most common reasons for failure is giving up when there is a temporary failure. Every person is guilty when he makes such a mistake at any time.

When you fail, the easiest and most rational thing to do is to give up which is exactly what most people do. More than a thousand successful men of this country believe that their greatest success has just had one step away from victory when they accepted defeat and gave up.

When you begin to think and get rich, you will see that wealth begins with a state of mind, a definite goal, and little or easy work. You and everyone else must be interested in knowing how to achieve the mental state which attracts wealth. Einstein was a successful man as he knew and used the principles of success. One of these principles is intense desire or knowing what human wants. Your right vibration attracts forces, individuals, and life situations to us in a way that no human being is familiar with; The forces that are compatible with the nature of our dominant thoughts. Before we can have lots of wealth, we must attract our minds with a strong desire for wealth and have a monetary awareness so that such a strong desire for money leads us towards finding new ideas.

Victory

Everyone who wants to succeed in any responsibility must be willing to destroy all the bridges behind them and cut all sources of retreat. Only by doing so, it can be ensured that the mental state of desire to win is maintained; The situation which is necessary for success.
But you have always heard that everyone advises not to destroy the bridges behind you. As you think you have a way to return, you do not try hard to succeed. Money is the dream of every human who knows it. Dreams alone do not bring wealth. What brings wealth is the desire to have it along with an endless desire that becomes intellectual pleasure; Then, gather your ideas, and get to work If you want the money so enthusiastically that is your intellectual desire, you will have no problem convincing yourself to get that money. The goal is to ask for money and be determined to earn it, which makes you convince yourself to get it. Only those who are "aware" of money accumulate great wealth. Money awareness means that the mind is full of a strong desire for money and the person can see oneself as its owner. All of those who have accumulated great wealth began with dreams, hopes, aspirations, and strong

plans before making money. You may have realized that you can never make a huge wealth unless you can have great excitement and desire to achieve it. In fact, believe that you will own it. You may also know that every great leader has been a dreamer from the beginning of civilization until now. Since the founders of that civilization have always been passionate dreamers who had the insight and imagination for seeing reality in its spiritual form before it became physical. If you fail to see the vast wealth in your imagination, you will never see it in your bank balance. While planning to achieve your share of wealth, do not let anyone affect you and humiliate your dreams. If what you want to do is right and you believe it, then go on! Show your dream to others clearly and if you fail temporarily, it does not matter what "they" say. Maybe "they" do not know that every failure brings the seed of equivalent success.

Thomas Edison had a dream of a lamp that could work with electricity. He began to make his dream come true from where he was standing. Despite being defeated more than ten thousand times, he still stood by that dream to convert it to a physical reality. Real dreamers never surrender! You have become frustrated when in the crisis and have felt that your personality has been crushed. Be brave because such experiences have set the spiritual material you have created. All of those who succeed in life have a bad beginning and go through a lot of hard work before reaching their goal. The turning point of the lives of those who succeed normally comes in the time of crisis. Having a dream is different from being ready to receive it. Nobody is ready for something until they believe that they can achieve it. Mental state must be believed not just to have hope or wish. A great understanding power is required for belief. A closed mind and short-sightedness cannot inspire faith, bravery, and belief. Use simple methods for focusing as if he has never believed in difficult things; Create a mind that does not know any word named impossible and does not accept a reality called failure.

Faith

Faith is the main alchemist of the mind. When faith is merged with the vibration of thought, the subconscious mind receives that vibration immediately, returns it to its spiritual equivalent, and transfers it to infinite intelligence; as it is true about worship. This principle converts intense desire into its physical or monetary equivalent. Such a principle is faith. Faith is a state of mind that may be induced or created in the subconscious mind by consecutive commands through self- indulgence. It is extremely difficult to describe the way in which human develops his faith. Currently, this method does not exist. In fact, it is difficult to describe the color red for a blind person who has never seen any color. Faith is the certainty of heart that can be gained voluntarily after trusting in God. Emphasizing the commands to your subconscious mind in an iterative way is the only way known to develop a sense of faith voluntarily. Every thought that constantly enters the subconscious mind is finally accepted and goes so far to turn the thought into its physical equivalent by the most available practical procedure. Your belief is the factor which determines the action of your subconscious mind. When you give some instructions to your subconscious mind with self-indulgence, no problem can prevent you from deceiving this mind. Understand this fact to realize why it is significant to encourage positive feelings as the forces prevailing your mind and to weaken negative feelings. A mind that is dominated by positive feelings has a desirable place for the state of mind whether right or wrong. If a person repeats a lie over and over again, he will finally accept the lie as a truth and believes that it is the truth. Now, a description of a considerable fact comes to mind that is that the thoughts which merge with each of the feelings and emotions and exert a "magnetic" force; Thus, a "magnetized" thought may be compared to a seed that germinates, grows, and multiplies many times when planted in fertile soil; This will turn a small original seed into millions of seeds of the same type. We are who we really are due to the mental vibrations we select and record through the stimuli of our daily environment. Let go of the effects of any ominous environment and build your life. By considering the list of mental assets and liabilities, you will realize that your biggest weakness is the lack of self-confidence. Such a defect and inadequacy can be converted into courage with the help of self-indoctrination.

If you think you have failed, then you have failed.
If you think you have no courage, then you have not.
If you think you will lose, then you will lose.
If you think you are better than others, then you are.

While reading the emphatic phrase aloud with which you try to develop "monetary awareness", remember that reading such sentences alone has no result unless you combine feelings or emotion with your words. If you say "I get better and better every day" a million times without feeling happy, you will not experience any desired result. Your subconscious mind only recognizes and acts on the thoughts which are fully integrated with emotions or feelings.

Simple and non-emotional words have no effect on the subconscious mind. Do not wait for a specific plan or program to exchange your services or goods for the anticipated money; Instead, find yourself as the owner of the money. In addition, claim and predict that your subconscious mind will give you the plans you need. Science will not attract money unless it is organized with practical plans and directed to a specific goal to save money. Not understanding this fact is the source of confusion for millions of people who mistakenly believe that "knowledge is power" but it is not true! Knowledge is only potential power and becomes power only when it is organized in specific practical plans and directed to a specific goal.

Accumulating enormous wealth requires power and power is acquired through specialized knowledge; A knowledge which is fully organized and intelligently directed but this knowledge should not be necessarily provided to someone who has accumulated the wealth. One of the weirdest things about human is that he only appreciates a situation that has a price. Awareness on how to acquire knowledge is valuable! A person who stops studying just because he has graduated from university is always doomed to frustration and remains as an ordinary person. It does not matter what job he has. The way to success is the continuous pursuit of knowledge. If you have imagination, this chapter may give you sufficient ideas to accumulate the wealth you want. Keep it in mind that the main subject is thought and idea. Specialized knowledge can be found in every corner!

Creative mind

In fact, imagination is a workshop where all human-made plans are renewed. Form, state, and action are given to intense desire with the help of imaginative power of mind.

It is said that human can make anything he imagines. If you are one of those who believe that hard work and honesty will bring wealth, clear your mind; It is not true! When wealth comes in large quantities, it is not the result of hard work! If wealth is gained in response to specific demands, it comes based on the use of specific principles not by chance and probability. Generally, it is an idea that evokes action by referring to the power of imagination. All skilled sellers know that they may not be able to sell the product but finally they sell the idea somewhere. Ordinary sellers do not know this; For this reason, they are ordinary. Success requires no explanation and failure accepts no excuse. No human being has ever been forced unless he surrenders in his mind. This fact will be repeated many times since it is very easy for human to be completely defeated upon the first sign of failure. A helpless person never wins and a winner never gives up. Take this sentence, write it in capital letters on a piece of paper, and put it in a place where you can see it every night before going to bed and every morning before going to work. This is the characteristic of those who have superficial knowledge and try to affect others as if they have high knowledge. Such people mainly speak a lot and listen very little. If you want to achieve the habit of immediate intention and decision, keep your eyes and ears wide open and your mouth closed. Those who speak a lot do little. If you speak more than you listen, you not only will deprive yourself of many opportunities for gaining useful knowledge, but also you will reveal your plans and goals to those who will enjoy your failure as they envy you. In addition, remember that every time you open your mouth in front of a scientist, you show him the exact amount of knowledge or lack of knowledge. Real wisdom is normally revealed in silence and humility.

Cosmic Laws

You must be rich because you have no right to be poor. Living and not being rich is surely misery and the double misery is that you can become rich as much as you can be poor. It is our undisputed duty to become rich in honorable ways. However, the honorable way is the only way that leads us to wealth quickly. If you are poor, you cannot feel happy. Furthermore, you should not be poor. Poverty is a sin. Hellish poverty is the product of human's blindness to God's infinite blessings. Poverty is an unclean, annoying, and humiliating experience. In fact, poverty is a disease and in severe cases, it is a sign of stupidity. Poverty makes prisons full of thieves and criminals. Poverty leads humans towards addiction, corruption, prostitution, and suicide. In addition, it turns innocent, talented, and intelligent children into criminals and delinquents. Furthermore, poverty makes people do the things they would not have thought if they were not poor. Poverty is the result of the current wars. Most governments that have fulfilled some work have normally done so for economic reasons and have considered this system as a solution to financial security. The sinful consequences of poverty are the burden of endless poverty. Do not accept any excuse for dealing with poverty or accepting it as a permanent situation. You will not be able to become rich just because you can do so many good things. The main reason you want to become rich is that you must be rich. As the power of creation has been given to you, wealth is your certain right and divine heritage. There is no reason to separate wealth from spiritual life. There is no need that you live in two worlds. Run six days a week and give God a chance on the seventh day to show you what He can do. Look at God as a wealthy and loving father who understands your situation and feelings and is interested in all your affairs and cares for all parts of your life every day of the week and every moment. Seek His guidance for all your affairs — whether financial or else — and seek His divine command. Then, you will be amazed at the pleasant improvement of all aspects of your life. The divine promise is: "Everything belongs to you." When you find that it is God's will for you to be rich, and as the Creator of this rich world, He is the source of your wealth, then you will not fall in love with wealth and will not idolize your wealth for yourself. You merely claim your rich and infinite heritage from the source of all your blessings. The word wealth means a glorious life and this is exactly what the thinker should strive to achieve and consider it as his spiritual right. If you consider God as the source of all your blessings and wealth and have hope in Him for every detail of your financial affairs, all aspects of your life will become stable. Then, a time will come when you will not see financial urgency and will not need immediate heavenly blessings. Surprisingly, the more you know God as the source of your livelihood, the better your financial conditions will become and the substance that meets your needs will always be available to you. Whenever you consider God as the constant source of your blessings and ask God for your daily sustenance, He will provide for you. Always remember that God is the source of all blessings. Then, make spiritual contact with Him and His rich essence that are waiting for your knowledge and approval and say: God loves me. Now, I accept all His precious gifts. My joyful success is God's will and such blessings of God will be given to me soon. It is amazing to know that everything can be fulfilled first on the mind and realize that your mind is your divine power that you can use for goodwill. The reason why everything can be fulfilled on the mind first is that the mind is the connecting link between the tangible world and the intangible world.

Cosmic Laws

We are all like magnets! As a magnet, you do not have to pull success towards yourself by force. Instead of wandering in distress, pressure, criticism, anxiety, depression, lack of forgiveness, and a sense of ownership that absorb all kinds of misery and failure, you can have that joyful mental position and the hope of getting rich that pull all the good gifts of the world to you.

Here, I teach you one of the "forgiveness" techniques that can help you get even more for every blessing you need right now in your life. Sit in a quiet place for an hour every day and forgive all those who have oppressed you or you have a bad feeling about them. If you have accused someone of injustice, if you have spoken angrily to someone, if you have criticized someone or have talked behind them, if your work has led to a legal dispute with someone, ask them for forgiveness on your mind. Their subconscious mind will take your message and answer positively. Forgive yourself if you have accused yourself of failing or making a mistake. Forgiveness can calm you down and open the way to wealth and success. In order to forgive others, repeat on your mind: God's forgiving love has released us. Divine love creates good and perfect fruits and then peace will be established among us again. I see God with a better vision and consider Him as the most merciful of all. Repeat this sentence to become rich: "I only seek refuge in God's forgiveness, grace, and mercy."
Are you thinking how to solve your problems? If you are in such a condition, let go and get free. You must give up something or someone. Repeat constantly about the situation or the people you are involved with: "I am free. I give up everything and leave everything to God." Do not be scared of letting go. You will not lose anything by giving up. There is freedom and deliverance in spirituality but there is no loss. Let go of the blessings of yourself and

others so that they move more freely towards you. Letting go increases the attraction power of blessings.

We all want to have a better financial position. Besides, wealth is our natural right. The way to achieve wealth is: Never talk about financial problems and poverty. Instead, think of the abundance in the world that can be found everywhere. Then, learn to let go, give up, give gifts and in this way, make room for the things you have prayed for or dreamed. When you throw away old ideas, tendencies, objects, and possessions from your living space and instead replace new ideas of wealth, success, and progress, your condition will become better day by day. You always want something better. This is a requirement for progress. As children's clothes shrink for them, you see that your previous ideals have shrunk for you as you expand the horizons of your life.

Many people attempt to become rich by external ways, but they do not reach their goals as they are scared to clarify their thoughts and achieve definite goals.

They want a better life and more money, but do not know how they want to live better and how much money they need. Many people are scared of certainty. They think what if they have set a task for God. When a right and strong desire comes to you, it is the hand of God that knocks on your door and wants to give you a bigger blessing. If you suppress such desires and do not let them be expressed in a constructive way, they will normally go astray and appear as destructively or as nervous tendencies, pressures, fears, addictions, mental illnesses, sexual imbalances, or other negative actions. God's promise is: Call me to answer you. Thinking about your dreams, expressing them constructively by writing, setting the desired time for your dreams to come true, and praying for God's grace have wonderful results.

It may seem naive, but typically big truths and powerful secrets are so simple that an ordinary person ignores it in an attempt to find a more difficult way. According to God's will, you should be superior in all areas because the kingdom of God is in your hands. However, if you seek God's help to experience this kingdom, the least you can do is be honest with Him and yourself. Otherwise, you block the way to any success. Another technique that is particularly useful for paying bills is to write "Thank you for providing your services to us" on the envelope instead of feeling hatred and disgust for them. As you want greater blessings, you must create mental images of them on your mind. Perhaps the argument suggests you not to care at all. Perhaps your willpower says that this dream is too big to come true. If you stick to your imagination, it will make your dream come true.

By continuing this practice, you will gain the willpower. Hope and expectation will create and manifest everything you teach your mind. In fact, you are always busy with your imagination; But maybe you used it for the image of poverty and frustration and everything you do not want to have in life. Whenever you sit quietly in a corner, hold your wallet and checkbook, close your eyes, and visualize that your wallet is full of bills. See your savings account with very large numbers.

Use your imagination. The power of imagination and imagination ... See all the goodness and blessings that you want to experience in your imagination.

Emphatic phrases

Nowadays, we constantly hear about "emphatic phrases" which are kind of command. Many have proven that daily practice of "emphatic phrases" whether loudly or quietly is the easiest way to awaken the command law for achieving one's dreams. Indeed, using "emphatic phrases" to create what you want is so simple so that not many people can trust it but look for a more complex way.

When you say "emphatic phrases" to emphasize your desired blessing and do not talk about what you do not want, you apply a new process on your mind to expand the emphasis in more spaces and manifest your desired blessing at the material level.

The more you emphasize your desired blessing, the faster you will see its results.

Never underestimate the influence of words. Your words make your world. There are hundreds of emphatic phrases that you can use for commanding your desired blessing. You must not hesitate to use them. For instance, if your income is not sufficient or your wallet is empty, take it in your hands and say it loudly several times:

"I ask for blessing for you and now I thank you for the wealth of God that come from you to me."

We have prepared the most complete emphatic phrases on our website, both as audio and pdf.

Visit our website and prepare the files and listen every day. Website address: www.moghadasii.com

When you eat with pleasure, ask for blessing and appreciate your food. When you get dressed, wear your clothes with gratitude and joy. They may consider me as an extremist in the use of the emphatic phrases. As you can find an emphatic phrase in every corner of my house that I have put on the objects in the house. I know the power of such phrases. I have put the emphatic phrases about health, youth, and beauty on my mirror. The emphatic phrases I have put on the bread container are as follows: "I thank God for the blessings which are constantly manifested in

Cosmic Laws

my life. I thank God for the infinite blessing that is manifested here now beyond my need. »

In order to prevent those who are in my life without any reason, I have put these phrase: " Divine order is established in my life right now." It is very great to begin the day by repeating the emphatic phrases which help you control your whole day. I suggest this phrase: "With praising, I send the infinite wealth of God before me so that I may have the guidance and support of God on this day. Whatever I need is now available." Awareness on the authority of wealth-creating thoughts alone cannot work. It must be acted upon. Daily repetition of emphatic phrases aloud is part of this plan.

How good it would be if the phrase "I have law" is used instead of "I have no law". People do not know that according to the law of the action of mind, they are invited to the same qualities when they criticize, blame, and humiliate others. Never waste your time thinking about reducing whether about yourself or others. Make sure that whatever you send out of yourself returns to you many times and creates the same experiences in your life.

Be full of the idea of increasing for yourself. Feel that you get more and more successful every day and help others become more successful. Every action and tone of your speech, as well as every look of you must reflect your calm and rich certainty of success. Whenever your mental world is full of deprivation, there is need to reassure others of your success by words because success is reflected from your being and everyone feels it subconsciously. They eagerly want to make a deal with you because they are attracted to the feeling of success that comes from you. You must only create a feeling of wealth, success, and deprivation in yourself so that the people with rich ideas that you have never seen before become your customers, authorities, colleagues, and friends. People subconsciously go to a place that is full of increasing atmosphere. The businesses which rapidly expand and bring endless blessings fall into this category. When you give others the idea of increasing on your mind and get entertained by this idea in the depths of peace and tranquility, others will be attracted to you and enrich you immediately. Have courage to awaken the law of increase in any way you can, whether on a large or a small scale. The spiritual essence from which the whole wealth comes never ends. It is always with you and responds to your faith, desire, and expectation positively. Our ignorant talk about difficult conditions does not affect it, though it affects us as the power to manifest us is under the influence of our thoughts and words. The infinite source is always ready to give. Spread the alive words of your faith everywhere to become rich even if all the banks in the world are closed. Return the enormous energy of your mind to "abundance" so that you have abundant wealth no matter what those around you say or do. Save and use the essence of your being correctly by focusing your thoughts, feelings, relationships, and activities on wealth, not failure or poverty. Let your thoughts and speech be immersed in wealth. Wait for wealth. Always remember that scattered and lazy thoughts, words, and desires cause scattered and lazy results full of poverty. Focus your mental images of being rich on the rich star of success and hold it there. If you get frustrated while trying to attract wealth, remember that it is easy and useless according to your previously beliefs but it is worthwhile to ignore the opposite appearance and think richly as it brings rich results. Learn to never be disappointed. Do not feel failure if certain things do not happen exactly as you expected or as you wanted. The reason why you did not receive it is that

Cosmic Laws

something much better is on the way at the right time. Add to your dream and attitude to witness the response that has never come to your mind. Failure is the success which tries to reach you on a larger scale. Most apparent failures are the foundation of a way towards victory! Free yourself from the humiliation of regret for the success of others and keep saying loudly or quietly: I do not envy of others' wealth. I ask help from God. I seek his guidance and become rich. There is infinite success and wealth for everyone in this universe. The golden rule of wealth is that you should never say or think about other people's financial issues that you do not want for yourself. Always repeat these emphatic phrases: "All doors are open for the whole wealth to flow to me. All doors are open and free so that infinite abundance can fill my body. Then, wait for it happily and let it come to you! Another point about money is: Do not be scared to pray for money or better financial status. If you have a financial problem, pray wholeheartedly for your special financial needs and ask God to help you fully meet your needs at the fullest glory. You cannot witness external transformations until the inside is not transformed as the inner processes of the mind control all the external experiences of our lives.

If you are stuck in failure and financial problems or restlessness and dissatisfaction with your job, none of these conditions should stop you from thinking about wealth and preparing for abundance of blessings and mental images for more success. If you seek step-by-step guidance from infinite wisdom in order to make your dreams come true, nothing can prevent your mind from advancing towards your goal. Dare to be the architect of your mind and build images of greater blessings immediately. Be happy of the images of your greater gifts as you run your daily business with courage. Seek and see your unlimited wealth bravely. It does not matter what is happening to you or around you right now. Say emphatically: "God, this or a better blessing will be come to me with your good and supreme will." Then, remember that you cannot improve your unpleasant conditions by fighting. Your conditions will not get better by blaming others for their frustrations and failures. Do not resist the current conditions and know that the transformation towards improvement has already begun. Whenever you feel that everything has stopped and does not move, remember that the whole universe is constantly moving and we are living and moving too even if we cannot feel it with our five senses. Nothing stops moving. Contrary to the appearance of the matter, everything is always changing. If you wait for better changes, they will surely happen to you. Put yourself in an atmosphere of wealth and abundance of blessings as much as you can and spend your time with successful people. When you try to convince yourself that a bigger wealth can belong to you, but you do not see any sign of it at the moment, it is time to take steps into the banks of your city and see the successful people who have lots of money in their hands. Now, it is time to visit beautiful and wonderful environments, as well as new and magnificent buildings and lovely shops. Go to the affluent neighborhoods of your city or to the very beautiful summerhouses, where the wealth of God and human can be seen. Take the courage to be different from all those who are immersed in the thoughts of poverty: do not think like them, do not act like them, do not react like them unless you want to stay at the bottom of the ladder like them.

There is enough space at the top for all of those who take the courage to free themselves from the usual aggressive thoughts, jealousies, humiliations, and criticisms which

Cosmic Laws

are common among many people. It is not important what others do, you ask them blessings, support and happiness, and show them your constructive and precious tendencies. Perhaps, you have not succeeded because you feel that you must do it alone. Therefore, you find failure easier than success. Recently, when I asked someone the secret of his success, he answered: Share God in your life to see what He does with you. One day, I decided to share with God. His guidance in my financial issues adds to my wealth every day. I begin and end my day by asking for clear and specific guidance about each project. I also ask for clear guidance on how to fulfill my dreams. Guidance always arrives. Recently, someone asked me: "By the way, how can you really meet all these expectations?" I told him: "It is very easy. God is my friend and I entrust all my problems, pressures, and difficult decisions to Him. He asked me in surprise: "Is that really possible? Can we really entrust great financial problems to God?" I answered: Look! If you cannot trust God, who is the absolute power of the world and is in charge of all these rich universes, then who can you trust? » Indeed, God opens a door where human cannot find any solution. One of the best ways to begin fostering and expecting financial independence and pleasant experiences is the daily, weekly, or monthly scale. It is easier for the mind to create immediate and short-term results. For instance, begin your day, even before you getting up, with a desire for abundance and wealth for the same day. Let your day begin and end with the thoughts on wealth. When you wake up and prepare yourself emotionally for the new day, or when you drink your coffee or tea at breakfast, write or say loudly or quietly a few times: "Every day, I am waiting for miracles from God for my life. Especially today, I am waiting for great blessings and I appreciate God for all such blessings. »

Prayer

Prayer changes everything. Prayer makes things turn upside down and go the way you want. It makes no difference what the problem is or what the cause of the problem is. Enough prayer gets you out of your trouble, only if you resist in praying to God. Be sure that God is always with you, in you, and next to you and hears your prayers. Whether your problem is that your son coughs, whether you are infertile and ask God for a child, or whether old hatred has caused a bitter wound on you, seek refuge in prayer that removes all bitterness and brings peace and tranquility. When you withdraw from the world to pray, it is better not to reckon about your failures ... Instead, relax and turn your attention to God and His Almighty kindness and mercy. If possible, let all the little concerns go away and focus your thoughts on talking to God. Keep the ideas in mind which help you. Very simple thoughts such as: "God, I love you, "God, I appreciate you", "God, I am in your presence", or " I am grateful for God's blessings". When you feel the presence of God in such a simple way, all your physical pressures will be relieved. Fear, excitement, and small anxieties of daily life will reduce. You can observe the fact that we are born with confidence in the actions and reactions of most childrens. I know a teacher who repeats oudly to his students before the class begins: "God loves me. God lives in me. My breath is the breath of God. I am the child of God and God loves His child. God always helps me". It is beautiful to watch the flourishing of bravery and self-confidence in his students, which is a reflection of his efforts. However, why should you have strong faith in your strong and deep beliefs? According to scientists, human is full of innate intelligence. Every particle of your being is full of creative consciousness. The air you breathe in and the world you live in are full of divine love that want to fulfill all your true dreams and give you all the knowledge you need. If contact this knowledge when you are full of faith, the same knowledge will create miracles for you. If you are unaware of the power of words, you must know that a beautiful positive phrase has the power of more than a thousand negative thoughts and two beautiful phrases more than ten thousand negative thoughts. Thus, whenever the thought of despair, discouragement, doubt, and fear of failure comes to you, say emphatically every day: "My power is from God. I am strong due to his transcendent power. All the powers have been given to me to acquire the high gifts of my mind, body, and affairs. Right now, I am calling all these powers to myself and experiencing them. » One of the best phrases which can be repeated at night before bed is: I go to sleep, but the God who is in me stays awake to solve my problems with divine order and lead me towards success, happiness and wealth. Another good emphatic phrase for creating confidence and self-confidence is: "God loves me. God guides me. God shows me the way. "You may never realize what effect your compliment can have on another life or what wonders your gratitude and kind words can create in another one's life.

The wonder is that your kind words return to you a thousand times over as whatever you send from yourself will come back to you many times. One of the most effective ways to create self-confidence is daily prayer. I also believe in this issue. Feel the kind God inside you and gain great faith and authority. I amm sure that you are now full of enthusiasm and confidence. The human who thinks can succeed. Always take a good step forward. Do whatever you can to let your appearance and inner be full of self-confidence. Try to always look like confident and successful people. Then, the thoughts of yourself and others will gather and move in the direction of desired success. Take care of the thoughts which take you away from your origin. When you think of judging or depriving a person of a particular situation, remind yourself that you are the best creature of the world. Try to replace negative thoughts with positive ones.

Make efforts to focus on life in the issues which reflect your divinity as you are a wonderful creature of God, a genius and a great creator, regardless of the judgment by others. Know that everything and everyone is full of the presence of God. Thus, be aware of the divine power in all creatures. Make sure that you will find how this force will secretly bring us mercy. Our origin is the Merciful God and we have given the eternal source the opportunity of attendance in our lives without our intervention. When you inspire others with the great goals on mind, your thoughts break down the barriers which stand in your way. The mind pushes the limitations and knowledge spreads everywhere. Then, you can find yourself in a new, big, and wonderful world. The asleep abilities, talents and powers will wake up and you will find yourself bigger than you have ever thought. Each of our dreams has its own vibration. When we foster such dreams in the form of positive thoughts on our minds, we resonate with the equivalent energy vibrations in the spiritual world: I want to succeed, I want to be healthy, I want to experience calm relationships, and I want to feel good about life. The energy of our thoughts specifies the level of spirituality in our lives; Thus, any doubt about our ability to achieve the goal due to the specific vibrations of each desire will cause the vibrations to be out of order. When this occurs, the barriers automatically come to mind. Thus, is not it better to foster the thoughts which reveal the greatness of our ability to understand our inner intuition? The thoughts which prevent you from revealing your abilities accurately question your worthiness to experience a divine life; Thus, they prevent the realization of our desires with the negative energy they send. Replace the idea that "I am sure that I will never get what I want, because I am sure I am not so lucky" with the attitude that "I will always look for the trace of energy I want with energy vibrations." Be careful with the thoughts which habitually invade the secret house of your thoughts and prevent the realization of your wishes. Thus, if you want to keep up with nature, begin a new plan so that you can see your dreams clearly in the mirror of your heart and walk toward it with small but steady steps. If you imagine that you cannot or do not want to do this, or if you feel that you are not ready for accepting them yet, I suggest that you prepare the books which can help you understand the issues. However, be aware of the vibrations of the energy in your thoughts and actions through which you communicate with God. One of the most effective ways of communicating sincerely with others is to use less of the pronoun "I" in your speech. Keep yourself quiet. When you want to interrupt someone in the middle of a conversation, try to remain quiet. Put the phrase "be quiet" on the canvas of your mind and remind yourself in those seconds that listening is more inspiring than giving advice. Use every opportunity to practice generosity. Try to help someone every day, especially strangers. I promise you that if you do so, you will experience the most beautiful feeling in your life in times of forgiveness. The more generous you are; the more inspiration you will give to others.

Show those around you by word and action that you are eager to share your time and money with them and make sure that you will become an inspiring person from their point of view by doing so. All humans are inspired to see someone give their time and money to others. Before beginning your day, spend a few minutes with God. When you wake up, tell yourself, "Now it is my turn to talk to God." At these glorious seconds, ask God for whatever you want, feel God in your heart, think of His greatness, and most importantly, appreciate Him. I normally say to God at the end of prayer: "God, I thank you, thank you, thank you! »

And what happens if you were told that your life experiences were mainly the result of your dominant thoughts, and that the nature of the thoughts you focused on became a reality? The phrases in line with such thoughts are: "What I was afraid of came to me" or "It happened as you thought it would", " Birds of a feather flock together. and "Whatever you plant, you can harvest the same".

Frequency

As you screen your life experiences every day, you constantly reflect the frequency of your dreams to the outside world, which we call vibration. With every vibration, the source that originates from inside of you and forms your immaterial dimension, focuses precisely on the upgraded version of life and when this endless process of life continues and you achieve new and improved results on your spoken or unspoken dreams, that wider intangible part of you will develop. The better you feel, the more you link susch frequencies, and the worse you feel, the more

Cosmic Laws

you show resistence to it. When you feel love, happiness or any other positive feeling in you, in fact you reach the pure moments of your life. When fear, anger, frustration, or any other negative feelings overwhelm you, it means that what you are think at that moment is against your will and you do not let yourself to become what your nature has become. Use the five physical senses to understand your environment and create new desires consecutively. The immaterial part of you which is still immaterially focused sees your new dream and focuses on it. Throughout the day, your material life experience lets you develop and create new dreams with every interaction you have with other people, everything you read, everything you see, and the experiences you gain and continue this process. When someone acts rudely to you, you wish others were kinder. When they misunderstand you, you feel like you want to be understood. Life makes you constantly grow. In other words, your standards and perceptions will become a better you as your non-physical part is always becoming what you want to be. The feelings you feel at every moment of life show your frequency relationship with yourself. Your feelings tell you whether the thought which has occupied your mind at the moment and the frequency with which it arises correspond to the frequency of what your source has fostered or not. When energies match or are close to each other, you feel great. However, you do not feel well when the energies do not match; Thus, knowing your feelings is necessary for your daily guidance. You need to find a way to align with what life makes you and enjoy the happy life you were born to experience. When you set the frequency, every action is inspired to you makes you feel wonderful. Without setting the frequency, any action you take will be highly difficult. By setting the frequency, every effort you make will result in wonderful results or save you time. Without setting the frequency, the result of your efforts will be disappointing. Finally, you will think, "This does not work for me. The law of attraction is the most powerful law in the universe which directs the frequency of the entire universe, visible or invisible, tangible or intangible, electronic or material, physical or non-physical.

The universe is not only affected by the law of attraction, but also by the powerful law of universe. In simple terms, the law believes: "Everything attracts what is inherently similar to it." »

For example, when you are proud of yourself, the feeling you experience indicates that the frequency of the thoughts in you is the same as the frequency of the thoughts which you are thinking at that moment. When you feel embarrassed, such feelings indicate that your current thoughts are highly different from the thoughts which have a broader dimension to you. You must let yourself become the creature that life has made you to feel happy. If you do not feel happy, you will not really let yourself enjoy what life has offered you.

But if you could reach the concept that everything you see around you was first a frequency of thought, and then that thought has formed and appeared in its current form, not only you will gain a clearer idea of how the real-life experience of the image is formed, but also you will feel the flow that is the source of the whole universe. We like the example of you sand your rowing boat on the river as it points to the futility of rowing in the opposite direction. Understanding the isuse that you can easily get what you want automatically puts you in the right direction, and as soon as you understand this, natural health and well-being

Cosmic Laws

will come to you and you will join the flow. The art is to let yourself become what life is made of. The law of attraction is not something you must follow as it exists in every particle of the universe. Just as the law of gravity which does not need to be enforced, but always responds to everyting consistently, so does the law of attraction.

The law of attraction simply sends you an accurate answer in thousands of different ways based on the frequency you send. Everything that happens to you is perfectly in line with the current frequency in you. The feelings you have inside you express the state of the frequency in you. There is also a much simpler way, i.e. understanding and applying the art of acceptance. In this method, you direct your thoughts in the general direction of your desires consciously and slowly and when you understand this powerful flow of life, youwill gain a vision of the bigger image of who you really are. Most importantly, you will be convinced that you need to reconnect with your true self.

In that time, acceptance finds a different nature to you. Imagine lying down in your boat and feeling yourself spinning to the flow of water; Then you think that this flow will direct you to the inevitable happiness and the realization of your dreams.

If you accept that the source within you is now in line with the frequency of everything you become and based on the law of attraction, you attract the most distant desire you call upon, then you will understand the power of flow. When you specify when and how your physical condition improves, you will prevent your recovery because you do not know the answer to your questions and create resistance in the frequency. In sumamry, although you cannot improve your physical condition immediately, you can improve your feelings that is enough. Creating means letting and accepting what you want to occur and knowing that acceptance happens through energy alignment not through action. What you do does not matter, but the frequency is important. It is not your action that makes you different, but the frequency. What you do does not make any difference, but how you feel about it matters. The key to create your desires is to find a way to turn your thoughts towards better feeling. Even if the current conditions upset you, you must use your willpower and focus your thoughts on what you really want and who you really are instead of acting in the opposite direction.

Remember that you do not have the responsibility of fixing everything. Just find an idea which makes you feel a little better. All this is related to frequency alignment. Do not look for measurable physical results. Instead, look for imporving your spirit and feelings. Whenever you feel better, you are more in line. In such conditions, the rest will come. This is the law. By looking around, you will see countless subjects over which you have no control. Thus, if you learn to focus your thoughts in a direction which is in line with the frequency of your nature, then you will be in line with yourself, and you will not only feel better about that alignment, but also you will send a powerful and coherent frequency to which the law of attraction answers. The intentions of others are nor important because even if they are malicious to you, you cannot overcome the powerful streams of alignment that you have achieved. When you are in line with your nature and are always in this situation, you will experience only what you think is good. In order to help your friends, you need to see the positive aspects of them and you need to align with your true nature and to be able to see the positive aspects of your friends. If you use this feeling for a while to measure your direction and always attempt to take step in the direction of relaxing thoughts in line with your nature, you set the frequency to align with your desires in a very short time; Then, not only will you feel more financially secure over time, but also your true financial image will reflect those frequency changes gradually. There will come a time in the not-too-distant future when money will flow so abundantly and easily to you that it will be funny to you that you have kept it away from you all that time. Understand that as long as you do not like it, you prevent your frequency from being in line with your nature, because whether you like it or not, your being likes it. People often think that if their partner changed, they would feel much better but the story is completely the opposite. When you say, "If you change your behavior or personality, I will feel better," you are actually saying, "My happiness depends on what you want and can change your behavior. Thus, I am not strong."

The more you try to make others happy, the more they become sad as they become dependent on the behaviors of others over which they have no control instead of being in in line with themselves. You want to make your spouse happy and you find that he/she is sad about something. You do whatever comes to your mind to make him/her feel better. He/she is distracted by his/her inconsistency and gets better for a while. Your spouse likes this improved state and now you are in charge of for making him /her feel better. His/her feelings are now dependent on your behavior, he/she gradually loses his/her independence and this makes him/her less happy. Thus, the try more to make him/her happy but he/she gets even sadder as you are dealing with the misconception that you must make someone else happy. You spend happy times, your task is clear to you, you are lively, you feel great, and send a strong frequency signal of happiness because of your coordination with the wider sources. On the other hand, as your spouse wants to feel good and the frequency that you send is related to this issue, it affects his/her frequency to align with himself/herself.

In other words, due to your selfishness in staying connected to your sources of happiness, you could lead your spouse to your desire. Thus, all you can do is love others enough to get along with them and that is the only thing which makes them happy. Stick to your frequency balance and let the law of attraction work. Now, such thoughts are completely in the flow and you feel better. When you get familiar with how you are created, your frequency deposit account, and your emotional guidance system which reflects the direction of your current thoughts, you will no longer be captivated by the behavior of others. When someone leaves you, you realize that only one person has left your life and this is not the end of your dreams, the end of creation, or the end of life, but it is another experience which makes you understand more clearly what you want or do not want. Now you have found another opportunity in order to create a more pleasant frequency deposit. Your business is created by your thoughts, not your actions. No factor can bring you the worst as much as focusing on bad traits and also bring you the best of them as much as focusing on bad traits. You found the answer quickly and enjoyed the development process. In other words, details have not trapped you, but your disjointed energy has involved you. If you can focus on your disjointed energy and keep in touch with the evolving dreams you have for your business, you will attract more talented people to deal with the details you want to implement. You badly want to move to a new house in another neighborhood and your spouse says that he/she wants to stay in the same house. If you only think about your new house, your thoughts will become more in line with the frequency of the new house, and circumstances will occur in such a way that you will achieve what you want. Get engahed with it and explain why you want a new house and be upset that your husband does not even want to think about it. In this case, your daily thoughts will not be in line with the frequency of your dreams. By thinking about your husband's opposing thoughts, you have added resistance to your frequency and you do not move towards the desired result right now. The knowledge on the fact that you do not need to agree with anyone else to create your dreams will set you free. If you try to correct him, you will most likely focus on the unwanted aspects which enter your frequency and block your creation process, and you will get angry at your spouse for letting go of your dreams over time. Many people explain that their fear was normal. Therefore, they refer to the bad things which are happening in the lives of themselves or their loved ones. However, the reason why some people experience negative events again and again is because when the first unpleasant thing happens, they pay too much attention to it and then it causes the second negative thing to happen and so on. Whatever you really believe will be observed in your life. For instance, if you strongly believe in shortage, poverty and deprivation, think about it constantly and considerd it as the center of your conversations, poverty will not leave you and you will face many shortcomings in your life. On the contrary, if you believe in abundance of blessings and happiness, just think about these blessings; Talk about it with others and act upon such beliefs; then, wealth, health and happiness will come to you. Put your beliefs into action and see that wealth and health and happiness will come to you and you will definitely see what you believe in.

You are a soul with a body, not a body with a soul. In other words, you are not a material being to have spiritual and divine experiences; Instead, you are a divine creature dealing with material experiences.

It should be noted that 99% of your real and unique being cannot be seen, smelled, or touched. In fact, a major part of your life is something beyond this body. This part is called the mind, feeling, thought, or super consciousness, whatever it is, it is definitely not your body.

Resistance

Why might you resist this principle of universe? Resisting for security is a delusion. As long as you imagine that your being is summarized in material and physical features, you do not even need to check your greatness and the dangers mixed with change. Think for a moment. All of the obstacles in the way of your happiness and vitality are completely focused on your material and physical characteristics. As soon as you believe that your being is more than a handful of skin, bones, blood, and organs, and the infinite and cosmic intelligence supports your body, you step into the realm of transformation and keep up with the other steps of the process. From today, try not to use material titles for identifying yourself. I have not introduced myself with my professional titles for many years. When people ask me what I do, I normally answer: My job is finding happiness. Although this answer seems crap, many truths are hidden in it. I may do anything because I am everything. You are not a human with a soul, but an experienced human soul.

Thought is far beyond what you do. In fact, your being is influenced by thought. Thought includes our entire being

Cosmic Laws

except our physical form that drags our mind to this way and that way. You must think of something that exists not only inside you but outside your body. The quality of your life is determined not by the things in the world but by the ideas you select to create your world through. When your thoughts are properly fostered and internalized, they will finally appear in reality in the material world and manifest themselves in different forms. We think through images and such images become our inner realities. For this reason, as soon as we get aweare of the cause of the illustration process and take this step, we will attract unexpected successes. The current conditions of your life shows exactly what images you have put in your mind so far. From your appearance to the level of health and nutrition, the amount of wealth, relationships, and anything else which requires action from you are all affected by the images you draw on the screen of mind. All of the images you select are saved in the mind and you act according to the guidelines of such images and thoughts every day. You definitely cannot have any feelings without using thoughts. Your behavior depends on your feelings and your feelings come from your thoughts ... Physically, all of us and everything in and around us are made up of energy

Energy is emitted at various speeds and has different qualities, thus although everything may seem solid and motionless, it fluctuates at the level of its reality. A simple microscopic examination indicates that a solid object, although motionless, is alive with the molecules which oscillate at less than the speed of light. Believe that there is no such thing called failure. Do not forget that your achievements are because of the images you see on your mind. You never fail, you only face the consequences; If you attempt to kick the soccer ball a few meters forward and mistakenly deviate it to the right, you have not failed while you have faced a result. Whenever you use your power of thought and imagination to experience everything you have seen in your dreams in the world of awakening, you become one with eternity and infinity like the divine prophets and relate to what is beyond place and time. In this case, you will find and freedom in what happens in place and time. In the material world, blaming events and others is a suitable excuse for not pursuing our goals. We blame the world for our disease, we blame the stock market for our financial status, and we attribute out weight to the confectionery.

We consider our personality as the product of our parents' inappropriate treatment. In the realm of thought, the guilt of our failures and backwardness cannot be justified as we are responsible for everything. Our financial status, health and other aspects of our lives come from our thoughts.

If we believe that thought is healing and can bring joy in our lives and also add to the differences in the lives of others, we will penetrate deeper into the inner side to manifest the most positive aspects of our being. As soon as we consider the inner world and the realm of thought, we move to the more responsible part of our being. Now, look inside yourself and see how you will feel after taking more responsibilities. Think how you can strengthen your abilities in the material world. Two hours of playing piano can strengthen your ability in playing the piano. Hitting a number of tennis balls a day strengthens your ability in playing tennis; However, mental imaginations are the only tool for practice in a world without form and matter. Every night before going to bed, bring some images of your goals and aspirations into your mind to do mental training. If you wish to have a fit body, see your fit and beautiful body on your mind many times. Let your mind be filled with such

Cosmic Laws

images. Focus on this ideal or image many times during the day and give it enough positive energy to manifest as an objective reality on the outside. Work on your thoughts every day instead of focusing on your behavior. The value of work and time consumption and energy inside is a hundred times more than outside. Indeed, it is your thoughts which create your feelings and lead to your actions. If we are overwhelmed by the mentality of poverty, we will assess all aspects of our lives in terms of poverty. If we live in a state of poverty, we will spend all our energy in the direction of what we do not have and we will continue this lifestyle forever. The living status of many people are based on the idea that "I do not have enough money" or "When I cannot supply clothes for my children, how can I believe in abundance?" or "If I had ..., I would be much happier." As long as such people describe life with a mentality of poverty, they will gain nothing but poverty and deprivation. What is required to eliminate this unfavorable status is already available to us. As soon as we realize that we are part of this boundless world and wealth and abundance are at all levels of our natural position, abundance of blessings will be available to us in different ways. The first step to get rid of the mentality of poverty is to appreciate whatever we are and have; Thanksgiving must be expressed explicitly. Be sincerely thankful for your being, that is one of the miracles of the creation system. Be thankful because you are alive, you have eyes, ears and feet and now you are witnessing an amazing dream. Try to focus on what you have, not what you lack. Make a list of the names and details of the things you are thankful for: friends, family members, clothes and food, any money you have, what you own, and everything you need for making a living. Everything: refrigerator, carpet, pen and everything else. Focus on your gratitude for whatever you have now and think about the things which temporarily belongs to you before appreciating the natural system for such blessings. As you learn to be thankful for everyone and everything that stands in the way of your life and also be thankful for all aspects of humanity, you are on the way of overcoming the mentality of poverty.

Focus your mind on any issue and see that the same issue will develop in your life and appear in different ways. For instance, if you have a considerable amount of money when you are in debt and focus your whole mind on your capital, you can be sure that your capital will increase very soon.

If you focus your mind on disease and always talk about it to everyone, your strength will be guided towards the development of the disease; If you focus your mind on the healthy part of your being and speak about your vitality and health, health and happiness will be fertilized in your inner side and will bring good results at the right time. We act according to our thoughts and such thoughts become our daily life experiences. For this reason, if you significantly focus on poverty and scarcity, it will flow into your consciousness and will certainly expand this situation in your life. If you feel something is missing in your life, it is just because your mind is focused on poverty; Such thoughts create empty spaces in your life. Now, if you completely change your tendencies and expectations from life, focus on perfection, and believe that you cannot own anything, your life will flourish. It does not mean that you cannot enjoy the wealth you have accumulated or that you do not enjoy the privileges of your position, while the point is that the form and existence of nothing, including you and me, will remain constant. How do you evaluate your competence? If you think that you have little competence, you have the same competence. Belief in poverty creates poverty and provides the conditions for this principle to govern your life. This rule is also true about the principle of abundance. In order to achieve abundance, you have to do something that you enjoy. Doing what you love is considered as the cornerstone of your life. Satisfaction is only possible when you are honest with yourself. Honesty means that your inner and outer mood is balanced; If you hate your business or are indifferent to it, your loss will be inevitable to the supernatural as the behavior that you do with your body is inconsistent with your intelligence and wisdom in the realm of thought. Opposite standpoints can be expressed in the form of positive words and phrases and make you a supporter. If you convert your bitter words into sweet and supportive words, you will focus your mind on the potential force and change the conditions in a positive way. Whenever this process is implemented properly, you will soon find out that what you focus on expands. We have learned to think about the shortcomings and consider what we have and what we do not have as a criterion for determining the facts. Without a doubt, we consider the number of what we do not have as a criterion for determining the facts while the number of what we do not have is much more than what we have. They have not taught us that the world is rich of blessings for each of us. Feelings of shortage make us struggle to make up as much as possible and work hard, yet we are constantly afraid that we may not reach our destination. Regardless of your small property, focus your mind just on what you have. Use every opportunity to appreciate whatever you have. Even if you look for more wealth or you are not satisfied with your personal characteristics, do not neglect appreciation. Thanksgiving fades greed and focuses on thoughts and abundance. When we appreciate whatever we have, the notion of the universe becomes more generous and gives us more blessings. I have found that the more greed we overcome, the more blessings will come to us. As soon as you achieve something good in your life, remind yourself: "I deserve it." Abundance is the result of how you feel about yourself.

If you feel that you are significant enough to answer other people's questions and have get so divine that you deserve a reward, you will take control of your reward. On the contrary, if you do not consider yourself worthy and consider your abilities as nothing, you have opened the field of your mind to scarcity.

Always use emphatic phrases. Use any technique to attract abundance. Walls, mirrors, refrigerators, and cars are the most appropriate places to install and display your emphatic phrases. An emphatic phrase can help you crystallize your dreams. In addition, it helps to honestly put your thoughts into action, and it is necessary to say emphatic phrases regularly. Furthermore, you are a set of energies that fully follow the river of life within larger systems.

As long as you do not interfere in the work entrusted to you in this complete system, you can do what is planned for you. You do not have to do what you think is the planned task. You do not have to try to do what you think is your task. Do not forget that any kind of attachment to the fact that things must go this way is a kind of interference in the larger system. The more you can free yourself from attachment, the more joy you have. Even the things that you sacrificed nonstop in the past for achieving and eventually led to more greed. Now, you do not need the amount of the principle of freedom from dependence and abundance without much effort and you place the

Cosmic Laws

celestial energy in your being. Then, the miracles appear one by one and warn you that the more you forgive, the more you will be appreciated. Nevertheless, the performance of this system is perfect, provided that you do not interfere in its work and do not get in its way.

When you turn on a light on the wall, you cannot see the connection between the key and the room that is lit like the day. However, you are sure that there is a connection and you know the connecting factors are hidden inside the wall. Thus, we do not have to look at the connecting factors, but we just have to believe that there is such a connection, even if it is hidden. As a result, positivity is the main condition and basis for having the principle of interconnectedness. Every positive reaction in life leads to another positive reaction. This process is not affected by the law of cause and effect, but only the continuity of energy in all species and objects in the universe. By using your mind as the source of thought - that is the source of energy and the center of life - you can create boundless differences. You can take advantage of the alarming fact in your life every day. As soon as you get aware of the fact that everything that comes to your way and everything you feel or think is part of the continuity of the universe, you have freed your life from bondage; You begin to see that all steps of your life are as complete as puzzle pieces. You can be placed in your mind or beyond your body and look at your actions; You can get rid of anything that forces you to use violence, and be kind and receptive to everyone around you. It has been and will be perfect and you will give up endless judgement and your behavior will be peaceful. The standpoint that everything will happen as it is destined and nothing is accidental, and our current status is as it should be, significantly reduces your stress and your need to judge about everything. Now, take steps away from your body in the fantasy world and see how glorious it is to be part of a perfect example. Avoid misinterpreting any unfortunate event quickly but see what is hidden behind it. When you know that you are the creator of your own destinies in this interconnected and perfect world, you will not blame anyone or anything for your misdeeds. You will change your attitude towards "luck" with the idea that everything you give to the world comes back to you with a full energy.

Leave out worries!

What are you worried about in this interconnected and complete world? It is illogical to worry about the things which are out of your control as your worries do not change anything. Worrying about things under your control makes no sense as you can change the worrying status upon you will. Do not forget that the world is under your control. God has breathed His spirit into you. Instead of focusing on analysis, you can focus on composition and control your mind from violence to harmony. Combining means putting everything together to see how well the components of the whole fit together. It is through combination that you can evaluate the degree of harmony between you and others with the principles of the universe. If you want to walk on the path of higher consciousness, you must test your ability to forgive. Not many of us are fully prepared for the forgiveness process.
Thus, we turn to blame, criticism, and resentment and get accustomed to blaming others for the failures and slips of our lives. By forgiveness, I mean forgiveness for 100%. You must be completely honest with yourself if you want to be completely free from blaming others. For this purpose, first consider yourself responsible for all aspects

of your life. Say to yourself, "My current status is the result of all my decisions so far." Say: "My current status is the result of all my decisions so far. Your culture may introduce admitting guilt as a difficult process. You may say, "I cannot do anything"; My status was unsuitable in terms of time and place "; or I was facing an awkward condition "; " My family status is the cause of this misery" or any other excuse for announcing that you are not guilty. Now, it is time to throw away all these excuses and look at your life with a new perspective. In this way, everything that has happened to you is a lesson for which you must be grateful; You must consider anyone who has stepped into your life, no matter how much you blame or hate them as a master. Do not attribute your encounter with them to chance. The universe is perfect in every way with all its components including the tiny particles in the atoms of your body, as well as the bodies of the people you blame. In fact, avoiding judging others is avoiding judging oneself. Your need to evaluate the circumstances of others, not those who introduce you. Regardless of the fact that you may see other people's actions unpleasant, the kinder you treat them, the gentler you will treat yourself. On the contrary, the more you become mentally disturbed by the misbehavior of others, the more you will realize that you have to work on forgiving yourself. Even if most of the people violate your values and beliefs, you will refrain from judging them. In case of demand, you will rush to help others and by taking steps in this way, you learn not to be affected by the behavior of others. Do not forget that you become what you think you are. Start creating your new world with your thoughts and ask God to show you the way. Instead of negative thoughts, consult God at all times. There are other worlds and possibilities that you cannot see. You must begin a different reality! You must recreate your life because whatever you say, good or bad, the world assures you that you have received it. If you keep reminding yourself that you are a victim in your life, then you will repeat it again and again to find images in your life. If you say that you are not as smart as other men, not attractive as other people, or not talented as others, you are right because the world shows you the same things. Anthony Robbins has a book called Quantum Questions. He says: Change your questions to change your life. A way to ask question is to ask positive questions. Ask the questions which will be answered and make you feel better. For example, what do I like? How much do I love nice people? What else do I like? What can I see that makes me happy? What can I see that excites me? What can I see that I wait for in my mind? What do I have to be grateful for? What do I like to hear? When you raise such mental questions, your mind has no choice but to answer them immediately. As soon as your mind becomes involved in answering your questions, it will immediately give up other thoughts. If you have no control of your mind, sometimes it gets out of the road like a car without any break. You are the driver of your mind; Thus, take control of it and keep it busy with your instructions on where to go ... If you do not ask your mind what to do, it will finally knock you to the ground like a horse.

Why do I not achieve my goals?

Do you always ask these questions from yourself?

Why do I not achieve my goals?

Why am I not lucky?

Why was I born in a poor family?

Cosmic Laws

Why does God not help me?

Why does God not hear my prayers?

Why do some people earn money easily?

What is the difference between me and others?

Why is money running away from me?

Why do all my relationships get ruined?

Why do I feel lonely with all this beauty?

Where can I find happiness?

And thousands of other questions you may have.

You must know that there are laws in the world which are fixed and God mentions them in the Quran as a divine tradition and says you will never find any change in the divine tradition.

إنَّ اللَّهَ لاَ يُغَيِّرُ مَا بِقَوْمٍ حَتَّى يُغَيِّرُواْ مَا بِأَنْفُسِهِمْ :

Allah will not change the condition of a people until they change what is in themselves.

سُنَّةَ اللَّهِ الَّتِى قَدْ خَلَتْ مِنْ قَبْلُ ۖ وَلَنْ تَجِدَ لِسُنَّةِ اللَّهِ تَبْدِيلًا (Al-Fath-23)
سُنَّةَ اللَّهِ فِى الَّذِينَ خَلَوْا مِنْ قَبْلُ ۚ وَلَنْ تَجِدَ لِسُنَّةِ اللَّهِ تَبْدِيلًا (Al-Ahzab 62)

The first change is to doubt everything you know and you must know that there is no single reality in the world. The world is the result of your thoughts and the world indicates a different reality to everyone. Thus, be aware that everyone's life is specific to their own and they can recreate it in any way they want.

By knowing this, you will never compare yourself to anyone else. By the way, do you really know how powerful you are? Do you really know that God has subjugated the heavens and Earth to you and they are subdued by your will? Do you know how unique and precious you are?

This subject is mentioned in the Quran in several verses.

أَلَمْ تَرَ أَنَّ اللَّهَ سَخَّرَ لَكُم مَّا فِى الْأَرْضِ وَالْفُلْكَ تَجْرِى فِى الْبَحْرِ بِأَمْرِهِ وَيُمْسِكُ السَّمَاءَ أَن تَقَعَ عَلَى الْأَرْضِ إِلَّا بِإِذْنِهِ إِنَّ اللَّهَ بِالنَّاسِ لَرَءُوفٌ رَّحِيمٌ

(Al-Hajj-65)

Did you not see that Allah has subjected to you whatsoever is in the earth? And the ships sail through the sea by His Command. And He holds back the sky from falling on the earth except with His Permission. Most surely Allah is, Full of Kindness, Most Merciful for mankind.

أَلَمْ تَرَوْا أَنَّ اللَّهَ سَخَّرَ لَكُم مَّا فِى السَّمَاوَاتِ وَمَا فِى الْأَرْضِ وَأَسْبَغَ عَلَيْكُمْ نِعَمَهُ ظَاهِرَةً وَبَاطِنَةً وَمِنَ النَّاسِ مَن يُجَادِلُ فِى اللَّهِ بِغَيْرِ عِلْمٍ وَلَا هُدًى وَلَا كِتَابٍ مُّنِيرٍ

(Luqman-20)

Do you not see that Allah has disposed for you whatever there is in the heavens and whatever there is in the earth and He has showered upon you His blessings, the outward, and the inward? Yet among the people are those who dispute concerning Allah without any knowledge or guidance or an illuminating scripture.

يَا أَيُّهَا الَّذِينَ آمَنُوا إِذَا نَاجَيْتُمُ الرَّسُولَ فَقَدِّمُوا بَيْنَ يَدَىْ نَجْوَاكُمْ صَدَقَةً ذَٰلِكَ خَيْرٌ لَّكُمْ وَأَطْهَرُ فَإِن لَّمْ تَجِدُوا فَإِنَّ اللَّهَ غَفُورٌ رَّحِيمٌ

ءَأَشْفَقْتُمْ أَنْ تُقَدِّمُوا بَيْنَ يَدَىْ نَجْوَاكُمْ صَدَقَاتٍ فَإِذْ لَمْ تَفْعَلُوا وَتَابَ اللهُ عَلَيْكُمْ فَأَقِيمُوا الصَّلَاةَ وَآتُوا الزَّكَاةَ وَأَطِيعُوا اللهَ وَرَسُولَهُ وَاللهُ خَبِيرٌ بِمَا تَعْمَلُونَ

(Al-Mujadila- 12 and 13)

O you who believe, when you consult the Messenger in private, then offer something in charity before your consultation. That is better for you and purer. But if you find nothing (to offer), then Allah is Most-Forgiving, Very-Merciful. Have you become afraid of offering charities before your consultation? So when you did not do so, and Allah has forgiven you, then establish Salāh, and pay Zakāh, and obey Allah and His Messenger. And Allah is well aware of what you do.

وَسَخَّرَ لَكُمُ الشَّمْسَ وَالْقَمَرَ دَآئِبَيْنِ وَسَخَّرَ لَكُمُ اللَّيْلَ وَالنَّهَارَ

(Ibrahim-33)

And He hath subjected for you the sun and the moon, two constant toils; and He hath subjected for you the night and the day.

وَسَخَّرَ لَكُمُ اللَّيْلَ وَالنَّهَارَ وَالشَّمْسَ وَالْقَمَرَ وَالنُّجُومُ مُسَخَّرَاتٌ بِأَمْرِهِ إِنَّ فِى ذَلِكَ لَآيَاتٍ لِقَوْمٍ يَعْقِلُونَ

(al-Nahl-12)

And He has subjected to you the night and the day, the sun and the moon, and the stars by His Command. Most surely there are Verses (proofs) in this for a people who use their intelligence

Sign and inspiration

Do you know how God talks to you? Did you always pray and say, God, why do you not answer my prayers? How sad were you and also sometimes your heart broke and you cried? Sometimes you got angry and did not talk to Him for a few days. But God talks to His servants. He talks to you with signs and inspirations. God swears by His greatest signs seven times in the Holy Quran and tells us about intuition.

1. Swearing by the sun and its light
2. Swearing by the moon as it follows the sun
3. Swearing by the day as lightens Earth
4. Swearing by the night as it covers the light
5. Swearing by the sky and the one who created it
6. Swearing by Earth and the one who created it
7. Swearing to breath and the one who made it

God swears so many times to say that good and bad are inspired to everyone every moment. Your feelings receive these inspirations. It is only your senses that can understand this point. If you learn how to follow your feelings, you will never make a mistake and He will guide you. All your efforts in life must be aimed at keeping your feelings good constantly. Listen to happy songs and dance as much as you can. God says in the Quran: Be happy with my grace and mercy as it is better than all that you have gathered. It is happiness and hope that push you forward. The world rejects depressed people. The world has nothing to do with depressed ones. If you know the rules of this world, your work will go easily and you will have no stress or anxiety. Believe in yourself to achieve all your goals.

Cosmic Laws

Read the laws again and again to let them penetrate deeply into your soul and use them.

The law of belief

The most basic law that you must understand and work on is your beliefs as they create quick differences in your life. What is belief? Everything we see and repeat it again and again becomes a belief; Whatever we believe will form our lives. The very significant point is that whatever you believe happens. In fact, the belief is so strong that it attracts all the same thoughts and you become convinced that it is the reality of everyone's life. It should be noted that 7000strands of thought pass through our minds every second and we only pay attention to those that we strongly believe to happen. Beliefs are highly powerful. There is a quote from Anthony Robbins: Human is the machine of proving his beliefs, i.e. you do the things which you already believed in. Sometimes, beliefs make us feel frustrated. For example, there is no reason why we cannot do what we did many times but failed. However, most people make a mistake at this point. What is belief? It is the thought which has been repeated many times. Beliefs are highly limiting. They are formed during the first years of life. What you learn from your parents, society, and school becomes a belief and is saved in your unconscious and governs your life like a recorded program. Now the question is, what should we do? The unconscious does its job. The solution is to start thinking positively and consciously and clear the mind of previous data. If you retrain this unconscious, you do not need to work hard and it will work for you.

According to Bill Gates, positive thoughts make money easily. The more time you spend on training your mind; the less effort you will make for earning money. Dr.

Wayne Dyer said: "Believe to see". However, most people do the opposite and say show me to believe, i.e. he cannot believe anything until he sees it. If you were supposed to choose between optimism and realism, choose optimism to train your mind this way. In fact, realistic people are pessimistic. The characteristics of realistic people are considering problems as eternal, considering problems as very seriously, regarding problems personal, and they get destroyed with a small problem. You must constantly control your unconscious and thoughts ... Whenever you realize that your thoughts are negative, go back quickly and think positively. Sometimes people ask, "What is wrong with thinking negatively for a few minutes?" I have to say that such thoughts are gradually gathered and become a strong belief that is highly difficult to change. Beliefs deprive you of the thinking power. Your beliefs are more significant than your abilities. At Microsoft, a thousand people are better than Bill Gates, but it is only he who believes that he can have Microsoft. The best employees are working for him. Wrong beliefs reduce your ability and right beliefs take you everywhere Not everything we see outside is necessarily true. We can question all of them. For instance, when we see that someone works hard and earns money, not everyone is necessarily like that. If you believe everything, you will see more of it in the world outside. Pay more attention to the things you like to see more of. Human is the machine of proving his beliefs. Anthony Robbins. Belief in the inability to do some things is the most dangerous belief in the world that can destroy you.

We have the beliefs which do not let us do certain things, i.e. we believed that we could not do certain things and we would never do anything. Some people always compare themselves to successful people and say: he is different from me, he had a rich father, he was lucky, he was highly educated, his family supported him, and he talks about thousands of reasons to do nothing.

In fact, he acts on his beliefs and lives the same routine as long as he does not change his beliefs consciously. There is no limit in life but the only limit is what we have defined in our minds.

Poverty and wealth both come from our minds. Napoleon Hill

The most significant thing that most people do not know is that everything that happens in our lives, even the people who come into our lives, or even the ideas which come to our minds, are all originated from beliefs. Most people either do not know or cannot accept this issue. For this reason, they are neither happy nor rich.

How are beliefs created?

Beliefs are internalized in the human mind until the age of seven and control all human behaviors until the end of life, unless we want to change them consciously. Beliefs come to our minds in different ways, which are:

1. Family
2. Society
3. Media such as television, radio, satellite, newspapers
4. School and university
5. Work or emotional failures
6. Friends and words of people
7. Rational and logical beliefs
8. Objective beliefs

Many of our beliefs are affected by the words of those with whom we communicate the most, especially friends, family, and relatives.

Imagine you always talk to your friends about the issue that there is no good girl or a good boy or you talk about betrayal and then you gradually believe that no one can be trusted anymore.

As a result, your attitude towards the people around you will change and the world has to show you more of what you have believed. Then, you are placed in an orbit that is just about divorce, betrayal, mistrust, and so on and the belief that there is no longer any trusted person is formed in you.

How can we find our limiting beliefs?

The first step to improve beliefs and find them is to ask questions; In other words, for whatever we want to do, we ask ourselves the questions as: what prevents me from doing this?

Why can I not start? What are the barriers? Each answer you give to these questions determines your limiting beliefs. The technique of asking always works. Make and keep a list of your answers. Here, I will tell you how to destroy such limiting beliefs. You need to replace the old beliefs gradually with positive and new ones.

How should we create positive beliefs?

The first thing we must do is control the inputs of the mind. Most of the mind inputs are from seeing and listening and we must take control of the inputs and give our minds new and healthy inputs.

The solutions that I suggest are highly effective.

1. Turn off the TV

The first thing that you must eliminate from your life is television and social media. Most malicious inputs come from such sources. What you watch in films about murder, love failure, frustration, poverty, theft, imprisonment, death, disease, drugs, plane crash, wrong policies, war, hunger, and thousands of other things are carved on your mind and form your destructive beliefs. This has made people more nervous and poorer every day. If you look carefully, you will see that the poor are more inclined to use social networks such as Telegram, Instagram, WhatsApp, TV, and satellite.

Rich people spend most of their time reading books. They often get their ideas from books.

2. Stay away from those with a negative mindset

Stay kilometers away from negative people. They even find problems for solutions. Maybe there are many of those around you who constantly complain about everything. They know nothing but to nag and blame others for their own misery Do not argue with them to convince them and do not try to make them think positively as you just waste your energy. Whoever seeks something, goes after it eagerly. You must start thinking positively and watch your thoughts consciously. Try to see the positive side of everything. At first, it may seem a little difficult, but you will gradually. Positive thinking is like a small light which grows slowly and brightens your life.

3. Avoid political debates

Another big mistake that most people make is arguing about politics and politicians for hours and finally they are all annoyed.

How can talking about the mistakes of politicians and statesmen help you? It only makes you sadder and more dissatisfied. If you are a group that talks about politics or any other issue that you do not like, you can use the conversation change technique which means that you can say something and then change the subject. For example: Did you go to your mother's house yesterday? what was the result of football? where did you go last Friday? And thousands of other questions that you can ask and change the conversation. When you ask these questions, the memory of the one you are talking to will be cleared from the previous discussion for a few moments and you can now put your favorite subject on the conversation cycle.

How can we change our limiting beliefs?
Our beliefs are not created overnight or during a few days. Such beliefs are the result of thoughts, talks, and inputs which have penetrated into our minds consciously or unconsciously.

Leverage of suffering and joy

One of the most powerful practices to eliminate limiting beliefs is the leverage of suffering and joy; That is, we always escape from suffering to achieve joy. For instance, when do we drink water? When not drinking water is painful for us and thirst is considered as suffering for us, we escape from thirst and go to drink water that is enjoyable. This is exactly what we act in case of leverage; We must make something which is so suffering for our minds towards joy. Take 21 days for leverage suffering and joy and replace some of your beliefs with new ones each time. Say: not having money is suffering and

reaching money is a joy. Not having a good relationship is suffering and having a good spouse is a joy.
Not having a job is suffering but having a high-paying job is a joy. You can try the following techniques to change limiting beliefs.

1. Using emphatic phrases and indoctrination: By repeating positive emphatic phrases daily, you will replace your limiting beliefs with correct ones over time. If you are looking for appropriate emphatic phrases, please visit our website and prepare and use the audio and PDF file. Listen to audio files of emphatic phrases every day.
2. Using the model: Studying the biographies of successful people will help you re-plan your mind and get rid of destructive beliefs. For the convenience of your work, we have prepared a unique file of successful people in the world, that is available on the website. We prepared this file for the first time in the world and introduced the biographies of more than 180 successful people along with their books. Please visit the website and get them.

3. Controlling mental inputs: The conscious use of movies, TV shows, choosing the right friends, and staying away from those with negative mindsets.
4. Conditioning: Using this technique, you can replace your negative beliefs with positive ones.
5. Creative visualization: it is one of the most powerful ways to change beliefs but most people think that it is a waste of time. However, you spend time during the day and think about your goals.

Keep it in mind that beliefs are like springs, you pull them, but again they tend to return to their original form. You must continue until new beliefs replace destructive ones and you need a year for that to happen. Such beliefs are very powerful because they have been created over the years, but remember that you are stronger than your beliefs. Thus, keep going strongly. Beliefs are everything to us and are so powerful that changing them changes everything; However, the essential point is that we did not choose such beliefs ourselves. We have not even chosen our own religion. We accepted the beliefs of any land we were born in. The greatest effect of beliefs comes from family. If you were born in a poor family, probably you do not have a good financial status. If you were born in a family that have no good emotional relationship, it is very likely that you will not experience a good relationship. You become like your parents. If you were born in a family where the family members have been sick most of the time, the chances that get sick is high.

If your parents are obsessed, you are highly likely to be obsessed. Most of those who constant follow the news of war, poverty, earthquakes, inflation, and different diseases live in fear, distress, worry, and anxiety. These people normally have no happy life. However, those who think positively and are thankful to God every day experience an amazingly happier and healthier life. Many people say: we cannot put our heads under the snow and ignore the realities in life.

I must say that paying attention to the things you want to happen in your life make them happen. Golden Tip: Whatever you pay attention to, you invite it to your life.

Now, the choice is yours. You can pay attention to poverty, fights, crime, theft, war, and earthquake and experience them or you can pay attention to abundance and blessings and experience them.

Cosmic Laws

Conscious and unconscious

In a global study, Sigmund Freud (the father of psychology) and his students conducted an experiment on hundreds of people and obtained the same results. He realized a very significant factor in people's minds. He called this action the intelligent unconscious. Freud observed that everything we do during the day is controlled by one of these factors. He was surprised that the unconscious controls 95% of our behavior and only 5% of it is controlled by conscious. Freud likened the mind to an iceberg floating on water. The part we see on the water is the conscious mind, which is only 5% of the total iceberg, and the major part of it that is the main volume of the iceberg and forms our subconscious mind is underwater. If you pay attention, you will realize that every morning we wake up without thinking and do some errands automatically. A series of repetitive errands. Like washing hands and face, having breakfast, cleaning the house, going to work, we do and most of our work automatically. In fact, we do all this by our unconscious mind. We did not know most of these things and we repeated so much until we learned. Like walking, eating, driving, cycling, talking. Now, we realize that in order to do something effortlessly and easily, we must repeat until it enters our unconscious mind. Now, we know that in order to do whatever we want to do effortlessly, we must bring it into the unconscious mind so that it can be conducted easily without taking energy. For this purpose, we must fulfill two steps. The first thing is to give new inputs to our minds, and the second is to practice and repeat to train our unconscious mind. For new inputs, you can use our courses on the website and read the biographies of successful people and listen to the courses regularly for three hours every day and also use emphatic phrases. In addition, we have a highly important practice for you that you should look at the contacts of your phone now and delete all of those who are mentally negative from your list. In order to be successful, you need to be friends with successful and positive people. Remember to do the practices to get good results.

Heart is the place of the divine message and the understanding of God's frequency.

By the way, what does God mean when He says: We have sealed the hearts of the misguided? He says in several verses:

كَذَلِكَ يَطْبَعُ اللَّهُ عَلَى قُلُوبِ الَّذِينَ لَا يَعْلَمُونَ

Allah thus seals the hearts of those who do not know, (Ar-Rum-59)

أَفَلَا يَتَدَبَّرُونَ الْقُرْآنَ أَمْ عَلَى قُلُوبٍ أَقْفَالُهَا

Will they not ponder the Recital1, or are there locks upon their hearts?

(Muhammad-24)

لَا يَزَالُ بُنْيَانُهُمُ الَّذِي بَنَوْا رِيبَةً فِي قُلُوبِهِمْ إِلَّا أَنْ تَقَطَّعَ قُلُوبُهُمْ وَاللَّهُ عَلِيمٌ حَكِيمٌ

The building they have built will never cease to be [a source of] disquiet in their hearts until their hearts are cut into pieces, and Allah is all-knowing, all-wise.(At-Tawbah-110)

Cosmic Laws

أَفَلَمْ يَسِيرُوا فِى الْأَرْضِ فَتَكُونَ لَهُمْ قُلُوبٌ يَعْقِلُونَ بِهَا أَوْ آذَانٌ يَسْمَعُونَ بِهَا فَإِنَّهَا لَا تَعْمَى الْأَبْصَارُ وَلَكِنْ تَعْمَى الْقُلُوبُ الَّتِى فِى الصُّدُورِ

Have they not travelled through the land so that they may have hearts by which they may exercise their reason, or ears by which they may hear? Indeed, it is not the eyes that turn blind, but it is the hearts in the breasts that turn blind!

(Al-Hajj-46)

فَتَوَلَّى عَنْهُمْ وَقَالَ يَا قَوْمِ لَقَدْ أَبْلَغْتُكُمْ رِسَالَةَ رَبِّى وَنَصَحْتُ لَكُمْ وَلَكِنْ لَا تُحِبُّونَ النَّاصِحِينَ

So he abandoned them [to their fate], and said, 'O my people! Certainly I communicated to you the message of my Lord, and I was your well-wisher, but you did not like well-wishers.'

(Al-A'raf-179)

Heart is the place of feeling, i.e., these inspirations of heart and inner understanding are for those listening to their inner feelings. You must have had the experience that sometimes you had butterflies in your stomach and worried and then something bad happened.
Heart is the first place that notices external events. Now, we want to talk about another law called the law of feeling.
Good feelings = good things
There are many verses in the Qur'an that talk about not being sad.

قُلْ بِفَضْلِ اللَّهِ وَبِرَحْمَتِهِ فَبِذَلِكَ فَلْيَفْرَحُوا هُوَ خَيْرٌ مِمَّا يَجْمَعُونَ

Say, 'In Allah's grace and His mercy—let them rejoice in that! It is better than what they amass.'
(Yunus-58)

وَلَا تَهِنُوا وَلَا تَحْزَنُوا وَأَنْتُمُ الْأَعْلَوْنَ إِنْ كُنْتُمْ مُؤْمِنِينَ

Do not weaken or grieve: you shall have the upper hand, should you be faithful. (Al Imran-139)

وَلَا يَحْزُنْكَ الَّذِينَ يُسَارِعُونَ فِى الْكُفْرِ إِنَّهُمْ لَنْ يَضُرُّوا اللَّهَ شَيْئًا يُرِيدُ اللَّهُ أَلَّا يَجْعَلَ لَهُمْ حَظًّا فِى الْآخِرَةِ وَلَهُمْ عَذَابٌ عَظِيمٌ

Do not grieve for those who are active in unfaith; they will not hurt Allah in the least: Allah desires to give them no share in the Hereafter, and there is a great punishment for them.
(Al Imran-176)

يَا أَيُّهَا الرَّسُولُ لَا يَحْزُنْكَ الَّذِينَ يُسَارِعُونَ فِى الْكُفْرِ مِنَ الَّذِينَ قَالُوا آمَنَّا بِأَفْوَاهِهِمْ وَلَمْ تُؤْمِنْ قُلُوبُهُمْ وَمِنَ الَّذِينَ هَادُوا سَمَّاعُونَ لِلْكَذِبِ سَمَّاعُونَ لِقَوْمٍ آخَرِينَ لَمْ يَأْتُوكَ يُحَرِّفُونَ الْكَلِمَ مِنْ بَعْدِ مَوَاضِعِهِ يَقُولُونَ إِنْ أُوتِيتُمْ هَذَا فَخُذُوهُ وَإِنْ لَمْ تُؤْتَوْهُ فَاحْذَرُوا وَمَنْ يُرِدِ اللَّهُ فِتْنَتَهُ فَلَنْ تَمْلِكَ لَهُ مِنَ اللهِ شَيْئًا أُولَئِكَ الَّذِينَ لَمْ يُرِدِ اللَّهُ أَنْ يُطَهِّرَ قُلُوبَهُمْ لَهُمْ فِى الدُّنْيَا خِزْيٌ وَلَهُمْ فِى الْآخِرَةِ عَذَابٌ عَظِيمٌ

O Apostle! Do not grieve for those who are active in [promoting] unfaith, such as those who say, 'We believe' with their mouths, but whose hearts have no faith, and the Jews who eavesdrop with the aim of [telling] lies [against you] and eavesdrop for other people who do not come to you. They pervert words from their meanings, [and] say, 'If you are given this, take it, but if you are not given this, beware!' Yet whomever Allah wishes to mislead, you cannot avail him anything against Allah. They are the ones whose hearts Allah did not desire to purify. For them is disgrace in this world, and there is a great punishment for them in the Hereafter.

(Al-Ma'idah-41)

وَلَا يَحْزُنْكَ قَوْلُهُمْ إِنَّ الْعِزَّةَ لِلَّهِ جَمِيعًا هُوَ السَّمِيعُ الْعَلِيمُ

Do not grieve at their remarks; indeed all might belongs to Allah; He is the All-hearing, the All-knowing.
(Yunus-65)

وَاصْبِرْ وَمَا صَبْرُكَ إِلَّا بِاللَّهِ وَلَا تَحْزَنْ عَلَيْهِمْ وَلَا تَكُ فِي ضَيْقٍ مِمَّا يَمْكُرُونَ

So be steadfast, and you cannot be steadfast except with Allah ['s help]. And do not grieve for them, nor be upset by their guile.
(An-Nahl-127)

وَمَنْ كَفَرَ فَلَا يَحْزُنْكَ كُفْرُهُ إِلَيْنَا مَرْجِعُهُمْ فَنُنَبِّئُهُمْ بِمَا عَمِلُوا إِنَّ اللَّهَ عَلِيمٌ بِذَاتِ الصُّدُورِ

As for those who are faithless, let their faithlessness not grieve you. To Us will be their return, and We will inform them about what they have done. Indeed Allah knows best what is in the breasts.
(Luqman-23)

فَلَا يَحْزُنْكَ قَوْلُهُمْ إِنَّا نَعْلَمُ مَا يُسِرُّونَ وَمَا يُعْلِنُونَ

So do not let their remarks grieve you. We indeed know whatever they hide and whatever they disclose.
(Ya-Sin-76)

إِنَّمَا النَّجْوَى مِنَ الشَّيْطَانِ لِيَحْزُنَ الَّذِينَ آمَنُوا وَلَيْسَ بِضَارِّهِمْ شَيْئًا إِلَّا بِإِذْنِ اللَّهِ وَعَلَى اللَّهِ فَلْيَتَوَكَّلِ الْمُؤْمِنُونَ

Indeed [malicious] secret talks are from Satan, that he may upset the faithful, but he cannot harm them in any way except by Allah's leave, and in Allah let all the faithful put their trust.
(Al-Mujadila-10)

قُلْنَا اهْبِطُوا مِنْهَا جَمِيعًا فَإِمَّا يَأْتِيَنَّكُمْ مِنِّي هُدًى فَمَنْ تَبِعَ هُدَايَ فَلَا خَوْفٌ عَلَيْهِمْ وَلَا هُمْ يَحْزَنُونَ

We said, 'Get down from it, all together! Yet, should any guidance come to you from Me, those who follow My guidance shall have no fear, nor shall they grieve.
(Al-Baqarah-38)

إِنَّ الَّذِينَ قَالُوا رَبُّنَا اللَّهُ ثُمَّ اسْتَقَامُوا فَلَا خَوْفٌ عَلَيْهِمْ وَلَا هُمْ يَحْزَنُونَ

Those who say, 'Our Lord is Allah,' and then remain steadfast, they will have no fear, nor will they grieve.
(Al-Ahqaf-13)

أَلَا إِنَّ أَوْلِيَاءَ اللَّهِ لَا خَوْفٌ عَلَيْهِمْ وَلَا هُمْ يَحْزَنُونَ

Look! The friends of Allah will indeed have no fear nor will they grieve
(Yunus-62)

وَأَوْحَيْنَا إِلَىٰ أُمِّ مُوسَىٰ أَنْ أَرْضِعِيهِ ۖ فَإِذَا خِفْتِ عَلَيْهِ فَأَلْقِيهِ فِي الْيَمِّ وَلَا تَخَافِي وَلَا تَحْزَنِي ۖ إِنَّا رَادُّوهُ إِلَيْكِ وَجَاعِلُوهُ مِنَ الْمُرْسَلِينَ

We revealed to Moses' mother, [saying], 'Nurse him; then, when you fear for him, cast him into the river, and do not fear or grieve, for We will restore him to you and make him one of the apostles.'
(Al-Qasas-7)

If you want to achieve whatever you desire, you must first be able to be happy. You will not feel happy if your desires are met.

You must be happy with your current situation right now to achieve your desires. Many people have achieved everything but are still sad because being happy is an inner feeling that is not related to wealth. Thus, choose to be happy and try to feel better every day. This is the key to achieving the desires. God asks His servants in many verses of the Quran not to be sad but be happy with His grace and mercy.

Wealth

All of those who cannot get rich believe that there is not enough money in the world for everyone or they have beliefs about wealth which have made limitations. For example, they say that money comes and goes, the rich have not become rich through lawful ways, getting rich is not spiritual, or the poor are closer to God. All of these examples are your mental barriers. First, prepare your mind to become rich so that the world can provide you with rich conditions. Those who do not like money do not benefit from wealth. There is infinite wealth in the world because God is infinite. There are infinite ways to become rich. It may not come to our minds, but it the reason is not that it does not exist. Do not think that you must work hard to become rich. Sometimes, a simple idea makes someone get rich. Do you still think that you should become rich with a lot of work and perseverance? Did anyone believe that you can earn about three and a half billion Tomans per day?

SNAP makes the same amount of money per day. See how much is it monthly? Do you know why it does not come to anyone's mind? One reason is that you are in a lower orbit and the other one is that you do not believe that you can earn such money. If you are in a low orbit and they give you the best ideas, you cannot become rich. All orbits must be passed in order. Some people ask if they become rich, they will turn away from God l? Who has created such a belief in you? You cannot even go to Hajj if you do not have money. Now, why do you think that the rich do not know God?

Does anyone believe that Bill Gates is a bad man and is away from God? I read somewhere that it was written that the rich are closer to God. Since then, when I think about that sentence, it creates a good feeling in me. The North

Korean leader has a famous sentence as: wealth is glorious. You can also see the difference between the two countries. South Korea is very poor and North Korea is rich. If you grew up in a family that was financially weak, their beliefs have certainly affected you. For instance, my mother was always proud that my father worked from morning till night for a piece of bread. One day, I told my mother: why do we not have enough money with all our efforts. She got angry as if a barrel of gunpowder was put on fire and said: You must appreciate his efforts, he does whatever he can, this is our fate. We must be satisfied with God's pleasure. I do not know why I could not accept these words. Why should our fate be like that? I had a very bad feeling. This belief affected my brothers and no matter how I tried hard, I could not change their mental pattern. I feel pity for them and I do not want them to try so hard and end up living like my father.

I told you in the previous pages that you must not argue with anyone. I do not argue with them based on this law and let them decide for themselves.

We cannot impose anything to anyone when they do not want. It is highly important that you want change and then God mobilizes the whole world to help you.

I saw this with my own eyes in my life. God says in the Quran that we do not change the destiny of any nation unless they change themselves. I am the objective witness of this verse. Thank God. The rich are very kind unlike what you see in the films. Why do some of you insult the rich when you see them or call them thieves? If you want to become rich one day, your mind will not allow it to happen. Because your mind will think that if you get rich, you will definitely become a bad person and thus it tries to keep you safe in this area. Even if you have passed half of the way, your mind makes you go back to the first point and read a lot of books. Read a lot about the rich to plan your mind and loosen its limiting beliefs. Do not speak about expensiveness, shortage, or poverty at all. See yourself mentally rich first and then you will go to physical wealth. The most significant question that everyone asks is how wealth goes towards them and how long it takes. I must say that there is no need to know where wealth comes from. We all have a lot of ways to become rich but when we find no other way, we get frustrated. You see a limited area with your eyes while God has as many solutions for problems as the number of stars in the sky. Please trust in God's timing as He will give you what you ask for at the right time. In any conditions you are, just try to feel good and go through the current conditions with patience. If you can wait, you will feel good but if you are impatient and say I cannot tolerate such conditions, you will send a bad vibration and move away from the destination. If you try to be careful with your thoughts every moment and think positively, know that the world will be in your hands. Napoleon Hill said: No human has ever been forced to fail unless he first surrendered in his mind. This fact will be repeated many times as it is very easy for a person to be completely defeated upon the first sign of failure. A reluctant person never wins and a winner never gives up. Thomas Edison failed ten thousand times before finishing the incandescent light bulb. However, it must be said that it was a temporary failure. You have a great opportunity to progress when you are young because you are energetic, fresh, and creative. Mostly young people in such a condition that they have to focus on their goals, seek to have fun, chat, and have a relationship with the opposite gender. They will miss opportunities to learn and progress before they understand. Your life is your only asset. See for whom or what you spend it.

Trust

Faith in God saves you from any dependency. From dependency on work, money, spouse, boss, and whatever makes you dependent. Your faith is revealed when you have problems. When you begin moving, Satan enters from every way to disappoint you. He raises the questions in your mind to convince you that no one can get anywhere with trust and faith. Get frustrated and you are done. Seek guidance from God at all times and seek refuge in God from the temptations of Satan. God says in the Quran: Satan whispers in your ears to disappoint you. Anything that disappoints you is the whisper of Satan. Whatever you ask God for, have faith and believe that He will give it to you. God will not disappoint the hopeful. Write this sentence and repeat it every day as much as you can to let it penetrate into the depths of your soul. Ask God for your sustenance e every day and consider Him as the only source of your sustenance.

Do not destroy your self-esteem for a piece of bread. For instance, if your spouse dies, do not be impatient and have faith that you have just lost your spouse. You must live and your sustenance is in the hands of God and He will give it to you from another hand. God says: Those who are pious will get their sustenance from where they do not think of. Give away from what God gives you in order to receive more. If you have nothing to give away, do it with the items or clothes you do not use anymore. Give away from the knowledge you have. Please do not sell the items you do not want. Give them to those in need and see how God will open the doors of mercy and wealth to you. Have good thoughts about God who says: I am with my servants' thoughts. Whatever they think of me, I will treat them the same way. What do you want more beautiful than this? Believe in God who is infinitely merciful, kind, and generous. Rely on Him safely. Nevertheless, rely on God and be kind to people and respect them as much as you can. Those who feel frustrated because of their sins should hope for God's mercy. God forgives all sins. Forgive yourself too. Start again from wherever you are. Be a friend of God so that you do not need to be friends with anyone. Do not doubt about God and love Him wholeheartedly because He loves you so much. If you feel sad, ask God for forgiveness and believe that He will forgive you. Sometimes, you feel sad deeply at people like your parents, children, friends, or those who have oppressed you. I want you to forgive everyone so that you can feel peace. Maybe those people never know that you have forgiven them, but you bring peace to your life. Hatred, revenge, and resentment are like a knot in your life. Nothing good will happen to you until you untie this knot. You may say that you are not in our shoes to know what oppression they have done to us and it cannot be forgiven. If you do what I want you to do, it is because I have done it myself before. I have forgiven those whom I have been unable to forgive for years; But since I realized that God forgives all sins and He has breathed His spirit into us, I found out that I can forgive too. I forgave and then calmed down. If you forgive wholeheartedly, tears will flow down your cheeks. Forgive to see the miracles of God in your life.

Wayne Dyer, the famous writer, had not seen his father for years as his father had left them. He looked for his father for years to tell him how much he hated him. He lived with his father's hatred for many years until he realized at the age of 45 that his father had died in a city far away. He bought a ticket to go to his father's grave and tell him whatever he wanted and show him his hatred.

Dr. Wayne Dyer said: I could only cry when I arrived at my father's grave. I cried for hours to calm down and then I wanted to blame him; But when I realized how he died alone and there was not even a member of his family to bury him, I felt pity for him. It was as if I did not hate him anymore. Nobody wants to die alone while they have a family. I told him: you certainly did not have any good conditions as you did not come to us. All my hatred of my father turned into love and I returned. Ever since I have forgiven my father, the doors of God's blessing have opened on me. I cry every time I read this text. I hope that you can forgive those who have oppressed you. Forgive to calm yourself down. Forgive yourself if you have done something wrong to someone. Do not blame yourself constantly. If you can compensate, do so, but if you cannot, give alms to them. Everyone makes a mistake. Do not think that because you are unaware of people's mistakes, it means that they have not made any mistakes. We all make mistakes to become perfect. We must repeat that the closest person to you is God. You cannot approach God unless you are with God.

Understand God in the depths of your being to have no need in anyone. No leaf will fall from a tree unless He wants so. The world has an order that nothing happens by chance. There is no chance. Everything is in control of His will. Since I became familiar with the law of attraction, I realized that this order is highly controlled. Pray. Pray a lot. Prayer is your conversation with God.

Many ask me if our fate is written, then what is the good of prayer? Dr. Elahi Ghomshei says: prayer is a departure from time. When you pray, it goes to before eternity, i.e. where they are writing for you. Prayer goes before writing fate. Prayer goes out of time and place. You will connect to the beginning where they order to change what is written for you. Prayer is the mobilization of the inner forces. There are forces inside us that come together at the time of praying to heal the disease and solve problems. You mobilize the forces inside you with the help of God. God says: Pray so I answer you. I see many people who consider difficult conditions for praying.

But I always say that people must pray in their own language. Pray as you are comfortable with God. If you are praying for rain, take an umbrella with you and it means believing that He will answer you. If you make a wish, believe that you deserve to receive it. Thus, pursue your desires with trust in God. Be happy with God's mercy that is better for you than whatever you have gathered. Be prepared for receiving your desires. Trust in God's help more than anyone else. Ask Him for everything. If you leave everyone, then you will see how God amazes you with His miracles. However, it is easy to say. We go to everyone and beg them, but when we get disappointed we go to God. If you cannot do something, leave it to God to feel that the burden has been lifted from your shoulders. Make an effort in life and change your beliefs gradually with what you have learned in this book to achieve whatever you want. God is the only window of hope that never closes. He is the only one who can be called with our mouth shut. We can even go to Him when we have a broken leg. He is the only buyer who buys the broken goods better. Also, He is the only one who stays when everyone is gone. When everyone turns their backs to us, He hugs us and also He is the only king whose heart is calmed by forgiving, not by punishing and taking revenge ... See God as a merciful and powerful counselor. Talk to him at every minute and speak to him in your own language. He is waiting for you to call him.

You have spent your whole life with your thoughts, this time let Him decide for you. Consider God as pure mercy. His mercy overcomes his anger. Begin your inner conversations with God. Tell Him I am talking only to one who is God. Feel Him by your side when you eat, call Him when you walk, feel him. For God's sake, feel Him to fill your life with peace. Feel God with your heart. Forget heaven and hell. Just think of Himself. When your being smells like His fragrance, you will feel the meaning of life. Let go of the strict God they made for you and believe in merciful God. Most people I talk to believe in the God they are afraid of. What can you say to the God who scares you? Believe in merciful God so that He brings abundant wealth to you until you forget everything and only want Himself ..

Health

Thank God for your health every day. As you walk, thank God. As you eat, thank God. As you sleep, thank God. Imagine that you sleep at night and wake up in the morning and see everywhere is dark. At first you may think that it is still dark or the power is cut. When you check everything and realize that you cannot see anymore, how do you feel?
Imagining this subject is so painful that there is no need to say the rest. See how much you have to thank God for your eyes yours. Thanksgiving multiplies everything good and turns everything that makes you feel a little bad into a good feeling. Do you remember that thanksgiving has the highest vibration? If you are ill, do not pay attention to your disease. If you are treating, continue it. However, put all your feelings on health so that your body is in harmony with health. I see some people who first start talking about their diseases or problems when they see each other. Not

only do they not feel better but also they attract the other person's bad feelings Why do you not talk about the pleasures and things which make you feel better when you start talking to someone? What a contagious disease we all suffer from! It is as if we are looking for someone to define the disasters which have befallen us. Either we complain about the conditions, high prices, or the bad conditions in the society. We talk about everything which is sad and about everything that we do not like. What a bad habit we all have. We complain every day and say why our lives are getting worse every day. If you have read the book so far, you should be the last one to continue this defetive chain of complaining. Make a pact with yourself right now to separate yourself from such people. Control the inputs of your mind. Let what is positive enter your mind. Find appropriate health phrases and repeat them daily. Find your negative beliefs about health and replace them with new beliefs. I had a friend that I suggested him seeing a doctor every time he got sick, but he said that he would get better and it was weird that he got better. It is not weird for me now because I know that he believed that he would get better and he did. I always tell those who are sick not to stop taking their medicine suddenly. First, work on your beliefs and when you are so confident that you will feel better without medication, you can reduce or stop it gradually with your doctor's advice t. I think that no one gets old unless they believe in the aging process. For example, we all believe that we do not live more than one hundred years as we have seen so much until we have believed. Now, if we see a large number of people living for 120 years, we will come to the conclusion that we can too. Keep it in mind that the facts of everyone's life are made according to their experiences. For example, one of my friends says that all people pays money back very late and every time he lends money to someone, he falls into much trouble to get his money back.

He insists on saying that everyone is pays money back very late. However, I believe that lending money to anyone will pay back willingly and at the right time; The reality of my life is that all people are good and you can see that two various experiences have created two realities. Thus, if you have something in life that you call reality, your beliefs are shaped by the repetition of a subject and you can easily change it by changing your beliefs. Change your questions to change your life. For instance, if you ask every day why I am so miserable, your mind will look for answers that will indicate you why you are miserable or if you ask why I feel so happy, your mind will show you the things which make you feel happy. Basically, all good and bad things begin with questions. Assume that your spouse comes home late. First you wonder maybe he is stuck in traffic. Then, you ask why he did not answer his phone if he was stuck in traffic. Then, you call your spouse and you get no answer.

This time you ask maybe something has happened; You keep asking questions and your mind finds an answer. The problem begins when you have a negative mindset that only causes a fight just because your spouse is late. If you learn to ask the right questions, your mind will give you the right answers. For instance, can you ask yourself what I have to thank God for? Why am I so lucky? Why I am so fortunate and thousands of other positive questions. You may not have all these blessings, but your mind will find your answers gradually.

The world is smart

Nothing happens in the structure of the particles in the universe. Everything is guided by God. We think that the particles in the universe are solid and inanimate, but everything is alive on a subatomic and quantum scale and is receiving and sending information to the universe. Everything in the heavens and Earth is praying to God. Look at the trees, how their hands are always facing the sky for prayer. Can you hear the rosary of sparrows?
Do you hear the sound of rooster crowing in the morning? If you listen carefully, you will hear the rosary of everything. Look at your hands, they are always in prayer. You can not even keep your palms open for a few minutes, they quickly return to their original position to pray.
Look at your hands right now. If you feel the presence of God everywhere, you will no longer feel alone. He supports you everywhere.

بیایید به اهمیت آب در قرآن بپردازیم. آیا خداوند به هوشمندی آب اشاره دارد؟

Let us consider the significance of water in the Quran. Does God refer to the intelligence of water?

يُسَبِّحُ لِلَّهِ مَا فِى السَّمَاوَاتِ وَمَا فِى الْأَرْضِ الْمَلِكِ الْقُدُّوسِ الْعَزِيزِ الْحَكِيمِ

Whatever there is in the heavens and in the earth glorifies Allah, the Sovereign, the All-holy, the All-mighty, the All-wise.

(Al-Jumu'ah-1)

وَهُوَ الَّذِى خَلَقَ مِنَ الْمَاءِ بَشَرًا فَجَعَلَهُ نَسَبًا وَصِهْرًا وَكَانَ رَبُّكَ قَدِيرًا

It is He who created the human being from water, then invested him with ties of blood and marriage, and your Lord is all-powerful.

(Al-Furqan-54)

يَا أَيُّهَا النَّاسُ إِنْ كُنْتُمْ فِى رَيْبٍ مِنَ الْبَعْثِ فَإِنَّا خَلَقْنَاكُمْ مِنْ تُرَابٍ ثُمَّ مِنْ نُطْفَةٍ ثُمَّ مِنْ عَلَقَةٍ ثُمَّ مِنْ مُضْغَةٍ مُخَلَّقَةٍ وَغَيْرِ مُخَلَّقَةٍ لِنُبَيِّنَ لَكُمْ وَنُقِرُّ فِى الْأَرْحَامِ مَا نَشَاءُ إِلَى أَجَلٍ مُسَمًّى ثُمَّ نُخْرِجُكُمْ طِفْلًا ثُمَّ لِتَبْلُغُوا أَشُدَّكُمْ وَمِنْكُمْ مَنْ يُتَوَفَّى وَمِنْكُمْ مَنْ يُرَدُّ إِلَى أَرْذَلِ الْعُمُرِ لِكَيْلَا يَعْلَمَ مِنْ بَعْدِ عِلْمٍ شَيْئًا وَتَرَى الْأَرْضَ هَامِدَةً فَإِذَا أَنْزَلْنَا عَلَيْهَا الْمَاءَ اهْتَزَّتْ وَرَبَتْ وَأَنْبَتَتْ مِنْ كُلِّ زَوْجٍ بَهِيجٍ

O people! If you are in doubt about the resurrection, [consider that] We created you from dust, then from a drop of [seminal] fluid, then from a clinging mass, then from a fleshy tissue, partly formed and partly unformed, so that We may manifest [Our power] to you. We lodge in the wombs whatever [fetus] We wish for a specified term, then We bring you forth as infants, then [We rear you] so that you may come of age. [Then] there are some of you who are taken away, and there are some of you who are relegated to the nethermost age, such that he knows nothing after [having possessed] some knowledge. And you see the earth torpid, yet when We send down water upon it, it stirs and swells, and grows every delightful kind [of plant].

(Al-Hajj-5)

أَوَلَمْ يَرَ الَّذِينَ كَفَرُوا أَنَّ السَّمَاوَاتِ وَالْأَرْضَ كَانَتَا رَتْقًا فَفَتَقْنَاهُمَا ۖ وَجَعَلْنَا مِنَ الْمَاءِ كُلَّ شَيْءٍ حَيٍّ ۖ أَفَلَا يُؤْمِنُونَ

Cosmic Laws

Have the faithless not regarded that the heavens and the earth were interwoven and We unravelled them, and We made every living thing out of water? Will they not then have faith?

(Al-Anbiya-30)

الَّذِى جَعَلَ لَكُمُ الْأَرْضَ مَهْدًا وَسَلَكَ لَكُمْ فِيهَا سُبُلًا وَأَنْزَلَ مِنَ السَّمَاءِ مَاءً فَأَخْرَجْنَا بِهِ أَزْوَاجًا مِنْ نَبَاتٍ شَتَّى

He, who made the earth for you a cradle, and in it threaded for you ways, and sent down water from the sky, and with it We brought forth various kinds of vegetation.

(Ta-Ha-53)

أَوَلَمْ يَرَوْا أَنَّا نَسُوقُ الْمَاءَ إِلَى الْأَرْضِ الْجُرُزِ فَنُخْرِجُ بِهِ زَرْعًا تَأْكُلُ مِنْهُ أَنْعَامُهُمْ وَأَنْفُسُهُمْ أَفَلَا يُبْصِرُونَ

o they not see that We carry water to the parched earth and with it We bring forth crops, from which they eat, themselves and their cattle? Will they not then see?

(As-Sajdah-27)

وَفِى الْأَرْضِ قِطَعٌ مُتَجَاوِرَاتٌ وَجَنَّاتٌ مِنْ أَعْنَابٍ وَزَرْعٌ وَنَخِيلٌ صِنْوَانٌ وَغَيْرُ صِنْوَانٍ يُسْقَى بِمَاءٍ وَاحِدٍ وَنُفَضِّلُ بَعْضَهَا عَلَى بَعْضٍ فِى الْأُكُلِ إِنَّ فِى ذَلِكَ لَآيَاتٍ لِقَوْمٍ يَعْقِلُونَ

In the earth are neighbouring terrains [of diverse kinds] and vineyards, farms, and date palms growing from the same root and from diverse roots, [all] irrigated by the same water, and We give some of them an advantage over others in flavour. There are indeed signs in that for people who exercise their reason.

(Ar-Ra'd-4)

أَفَرَأَيْتُمُ الْمَاءَ الَّذِى تَشْرَبُونَ. أَأَنْتُمْ أَنْزَلْتُمُوهُ مِنَ الْمُزْنِ أَمْ نَحْنُ الْمُنْزِلُونَ. لَوْ نَشَاءُ جَعَلْنَاهُ أُجَاجًا فَلَوْلَا تَشْكُرُونَ

Have you considered the water that you drink? Is it you who bring it down from the rain cloud, or is it We who bring [it] down? If We wish We can make it bitter. Then why do you not give thanks?

(Al-Waqi'a- 68-70)

وَتَحْسَبُهُمْ أَيْقَاظًا وَهُمْ رُقُودٌ وَنُقَلِّبُهُمْ ذَاتَ الْيَمِينِ وَذَاتَ الشِّمَالِ وَكَلْبُهُمْ بَاسِطٌ ذِرَاعَيْهِ بِالْوَصِيدِ لَوِ اطَّلَعْتَ عَلَيْهِمْ لَوَلَّيْتَ مِنْهُمْ فِرَارًا وَلَمُلِئْتَ مِنْهُمْ رُعْبًا

You will suppose them to be awake, although they are asleep. We turn them to the right and to the left, and their dog [lies] stretching its forelegs at the threshold. If you come upon them, you will surely turn to flee from them, and you will surely be filled with a terror of them.

(Al-Kahf-18)

وَإِنَّ لَكُمْ فِى الْأَنْعَامِ لَعِبْرَةً نُسْقِيكُمْ مِمَّا فِى بُطُونِهِ مِنْ بَيْنِ فَرْثٍ وَدَمٍ لَبَنًا خَالِصًا سَائِغًا لِلشَّارِبِينَ

There is indeed a lesson for you in the cattle: We give you a drink pleasant to those who drink, pure milk, which is in their bellies, between [intestinal] waste and blood.

(An-Nahl-66)

Cosmic Laws

وَأَرْسَلْنَا الرِّيَاحَ لَوَاقِحَ فَأَنْزَلْنَا مِنَ السَّمَاءِ مَاءً فَأَسْقَيْنَاكُمُوهُ وَمَا أَنْتُمْ لَهُ بِخَازِنِينَ

And We send the fertilizing winds and send down water from the sky providing it for you to drink and you are not maintainers of its resources.

(Al Hejr-22)

Verses of blessing

In several verses of the Quran, God reminds His servants of His blessings to ask us expand them by remembering His blessings. Thanksgiving is one of the blessings of God that enhances our capacity for blessings.
Remembering the blessings makes the heart happy and human realizes at every moment that there is plenty of everything in the world and then he does not get worried about anything.
Thank God at all times to see the miracles of the merciful God.

يَا أَيُّهَا الَّذِينَ آمَنُوا اذْكُرُوا نِعْمَتَ اللَّهِ عَلَيْكُمْ إِذْ هَمَّ قَوْمٌ أَنْ يَبْسُطُوا إِلَيْكُمْ أَيْدِيَهُمْ فَكَفَّ أَيْدِيَهُمْ عَنْكُمْ وَاتَّقُوا اللَّهَ وَعَلَى اللَّهِ فَلْيَتَوَكَّلِ الْمُؤْمِنُونَ

(Al-Ma'idah-11)

وَلَا يَزَالُ الَّذِينَ كَفَرُوا فِي مِرْيَةٍ مِنْهُ حَتَّى تَأْتِيَهُمُ السَّاعَةُ بَغْتَةً أَوْ يَأْتِيَهُمْ عَذَابُ يَوْمٍ عَقِيمٍ

Those who are faithless persist in their doubt about it, until either the Hour overtakes them suddenly, or they are overtaken by the punishment of an inauspicious day.

(An-Najm-55)

نِعْمَةً مِنْ عِنْدِنَا ۚ كَذَٰلِكَ نَجْزِي مَنْ شَكَرَ

as a blessing from Us. Thus do We reward those who give thanks.

(Al-Qamar-35)

فَبِأَيِّ آلَاءِ رَبِّكُمَا تُكَذِّبَانِ

'So which of your Lord's bounties will you both deny?

(Ar-Rahman-13)

إِنَّ الْأَبْرَارَ لَفِي نَعِيمٍ

Indeed the pious shall be amid bliss,

(Al-Infitar-13)

إِنَّ الْأَبْرَارَ لَفِي نَعِيمٍ

The pious shall be amid bliss,

(Al-Mutaffifin-22)

وَأَمَّا بِنِعْمَةِ رَبِّكَ فَحَدِّثْ

and as for your Lord's blessing, proclaim it!

(Al-Duha-11)

إِنَّ الْإِنْسَانَ لِرَبِّهِ لَكَنُودٌ

Indeed man is ungrateful to his Lord,

(Al-Adiyat-6)

وَنَعْمَةٍ كَانُوا فِيهَا فَاكِهِينَ

and the affluence wherein they rejoiced!

(Ad-Dukhan-27)

يَا أَيُّهَا الَّذِينَ آمَنُوا اذْكُرُوا نِعْمَةَ اللَّهِ عَلَيْكُمْ إِذْ جَاءَتْكُمْ جُنُودٌ فَأَرْسَلْنَا عَلَيْهِمْ رِيحًا وَجُنُودًا لَمْ تَرَوْهَا وَكَانَ اللَّهُ بِمَا تَعْمَلُونَ بَصِيرًا

O you who have faith! Remember Allah's blessing upon you when the hosts came at you, and We sent against them a gale and hosts whom you did not see, and Allah sees best what you do.

(Al-Ahzab-9)

وَمَا يَسْتَوِي الْبَحْرَانِ هَذَا عَذْبٌ فُرَاتٌ سَائِغٌ شَرَابُهُ وَهَذَا مِلْحٌ أُجَاجٌ وَمِنْ كُلٍّ تَأْكُلُونَ لَحْمًا طَرِيًّا وَتَسْتَخْرِجُونَ حِلْيَةً تَلْبَسُونَهَا وَتَرَى الْفُلْكَ فِيهِ مَوَاخِرَ لِتَبْتَغُوا مِنْ فَضْلِهِ وَلَعَلَّكُمْ تَشْكُرُونَ

Not alike are the two seas: this one sweet and agreeable, pleasant to drink, and that one briny and bitter, and from each you eat fresh meat and obtain ornaments, which you wear. And you see the ships plowing through them, that you may seek of His bounty, and so that you may give thanks.

(Fatir-12)

غَافِرِ الذَّنْبِ وَقَابِلِ التَّوْبِ شَدِيدِ الْعِقَابِ ذِي الطَّوْلِ لَا إِلَهَ إِلَّا هُوَ إِلَيْهِ الْمَصِيرُ

forgiver of sins and acceptor of repentance, severe in retribution, [yet] all-bountiful; there is no god except Him, [and] toward Him is the destination.

(Ghafir-3)

$$\text{يَا أَيُّهَا النَّاسُ اذْكُرُوا نِعْمَتَ اللَّهِ عَلَيْكُمْ هَلْ مِنْ خَالِقٍ غَيْرُ اللَّهِ يَرْزُقُكُمْ مِنَ السَّمَاءِ وَالْأَرْضِ لَا إِلَهَ إِلَّا هُوَ فَأَنَّى تُؤْفَكُونَ}$$

O mankind! Remember Allah's blessing upon you! Is there any creator other than Allah who provides for you from the sky and the earth? There is no god except Him. So where do you stray?

(Fatir-3)

$$\text{وَإِذْ تَأَذَّنَ رَبُّكُمْ لَئِنْ شَكَرْتُمْ لَأَزِيدَنَّكُمْ وَلَئِنْ كَفَرْتُمْ إِنَّ عَذَابِي لَشَدِيدٌ}$$

And when your Lord proclaimed, "If you are grateful, I will surely enhance you [in blessing], but if you are ungrateful, My punishment is indeed severe."

(Ibrahim-7)

$$\text{وَمَا بِكُمْ مِنْ نِعْمَةٍ فَمِنَ اللَّهِ ثُمَّ إِذَا مَسَّكُمُ الضُّرُّ فَإِلَيْهِ تَجْأَرُونَ}$$

Whatever blessing you have is from Allah, and when a distress befalls you, you make entreaties to Him.

(An-Nahl-53)

$$\text{وَآتَاكُمْ مِنْ كُلِّ مَا سَأَلْتُمُوهُ وَإِنْ تَعُدُّوا نِعْمَتَ اللَّهِ لَا تُحْصُوهَا إِنَّ الْإِنْسَانَ لَظَلُومٌ كَفَّارٌ}$$

and He gave you all that you had asked Him. If you enumerate Allah's blessings, you will not be able to count them. Indeed man is most unfair and ungrateful!

(Ibrahim-34)

وَإِنْ تَعُدُّوا نِعْمَةَ اللَّهِ لَا تُحْصُوهَا إِنَّ اللَّهَ لَغَفُورٌ رَحِيمٌ

If you enumerate Allah's blessings, you will not be able to count them. Indeed Allah is all-forgiving, all-merciful,

(An-Nahl-18)

لَا تَمُدَّنَّ عَيْنَيْكَ إِلَى مَا مَتَّعْنَا بِهِ أَزْوَاجًا مِنْهُمْ وَلَا تَحْزَنْ عَلَيْهِمْ وَاخْفِضْ جَنَاحَكَ لِلْمُؤْمِنِينَ

Do not extend your glance toward what We have provided to certain groups of them, and do not grieve for them, and lower your wing to the faithful,

(Al Hejr-88)

وَمَا بِكُمْ مِنْ نِعْمَةٍ فَمِنَ اللَّهِ ثُمَّ إِذَا مَسَّكُمُ الضُّرُّ فَإِلَيْهِ تَجْأَرُونَ

Whatever blessing you have is from Allah, and when a distress befalls you, you make entreaties to Him.

(An-Nahl-53)

وَنَزَعْنَا مَا فِي صُدُورِهِمْ مِنْ غِلٍّ تَجْرِي مِنْ تَحْتِهِمُ الْأَنْهَارُ وَقَالُوا الْحَمْدُ لِلَّهِ الَّذِي هَدَانَا لِهَذَا وَمَا كُنَّا لِنَهْتَدِيَ لَوْلَا أَنْ هَدَانَا اللَّهُ لَقَدْ جَاءَتْ رُسُلُ رَبِّنَا بِالْحَقِّ وَنُودُوا أَنْ تِلْكُمُ الْجَنَّةُ أُورِثْتُمُوهَا بِمَا كُنْتُمْ تَعْمَلُونَ

We will remove whatever rancour there is in their breasts, and streams will run for them. They will say, 'All praise belongs to Allah, who guided us to this. We would have never been guided had not Allah guided us. Our Lord's apostles had certainly brought the truth.' And the call would be made to them: 'This is paradise, which you have been given to inherit because of what you used to do!'

(Al-A'raf-43)

أَوَعَجِبْتُمْ أَنْ جَاءَكُمْ ذِكْرٌ مِنْ رَبِّكُمْ عَلَى رَجُلٍ مِنْكُمْ لِيُنْذِرَكُمْ وَاذْكُرُوا إِذْ جَعَلَكُمْ خُلَفَاءَ مِنْ بَعْدِ قَوْمِ نُوحٍ وَزَادَكُمْ فِى الْخَلْقِ بَسْطَةً فَاذْكُرُوا آلَاءَ اللهِ لَعَلَّكُمْ تُفْلِحُونَ

Do you consider it odd that there should come to you a reminder from your Lord through a man from among yourselves, so that he may warn you? Remember when He made you successors after the people of Noah, and increased you vastly in creation. So remember Allah's bounties so that you may be felicitous.'

(Al-A'raf-69)

وَاذْكُرُوا إِذْ جَعَلَكُمْ خُلَفَاءَ مِنْ بَعْدِ عَادٍ وَبَوَّأَكُمْ فِى الْأَرْضِ تَتَّخِذُونَ مِنْ سُهُولِهَا قُصُورًا وَتَنْحِتُونَ الْجِبَالَ بُيُوتًا فَاذْكُرُوا آلَاءَ اللهِ وَلَا تَعْثَوْا فِى الْأَرْضِ مُفْسِدِينَ

Remember when He made you successors after [the people of] 'Ad, and settled you in the land: you build palaces in its plains, and hew houses out of the mountains. So remember Allah's bounties, and do not act wickedly on the earth, causing corruption.'

(Al-A'raf-74)

ثُمَّ بَدَّلْنَا مَكَانَ السَّيِّئَةِ الْحَسَنَةَ حَتَّىٰ عَفَوْا وَقَالُوا قَدْ مَسَّ آبَاءَنَا الضَّرَّاءُ وَالسَّرَّاءُ فَأَخَذْنَاهُمْ بَغْتَةً وَهُمْ لَا يَشْعُرُونَ

Then We changed the ill [conditions] to good until they multiplied [in numbers] and said, 'Adversity and ease befell our fathers [too].' Then We seized them suddenly while they were unaware.

(Al-A'raf-95)

فَإِذَا جَاءَتْهُمُ الْحَسَنَةُ قَالُوا لَنَا هَٰذِهِ ۖ وَإِنْ تُصِبْهُمْ سَيِّئَةٌ يَطَّيَّرُوا بِمُوسَىٰ وَمَنْ مَعَهُ ۗ أَلَا إِنَّمَا طَائِرُهُمْ عِنْدَ اللَّهِ وَلَٰكِنَّ أَكْثَرَهُمْ لَا يَعْلَمُونَ

But whenever any good came to them, they would say, 'This is our due.' And if any ill visited them, they took it for ill omens attending Moses and those who were with him. (Look! Indeed the cause of their ill omens is from Allah, but most of them do not know.)

(Al-A'raf-131)

يَا أَيُّهَا الَّذِينَ آمَنُوا إِذَا قُمْتُمْ إِلَى الصَّلَاةِ فَاغْسِلُوا وُجُوهَكُمْ وَأَيْدِيَكُمْ إِلَى الْمَرَافِقِ وَامْسَحُوا بِرُءُوسِكُمْ وَأَرْجُلَكُمْ إِلَى الْكَعْبَيْنِ ۚ وَإِنْ كُنْتُمْ جُنُبًا فَاطَّهَّرُوا ۚ وَإِنْ كُنْتُمْ مَرْضَىٰ أَوْ عَلَىٰ سَفَرٍ أَوْ جَاءَ أَحَدٌ مِنْكُمْ مِنَ الْغَائِطِ أَوْ لَامَسْتُمُ النِّسَاءَ فَلَمْ تَجِدُوا مَاءً فَتَيَمَّمُوا صَعِيدًا طَيِّبًا فَامْسَحُوا بِوُجُوهِكُمْ وَأَيْدِيكُمْ مِنْهُ ۚ مَا يُرِيدُ اللَّهُ لِيَجْعَلَ عَلَيْكُمْ مِنْ حَرَجٍ وَلَٰكِنْ يُرِيدُ لِيُطَهِّرَكُمْ وَلِيُتِمَّ نِعْمَتَهُ عَلَيْكُمْ لَعَلَّكُمْ تَشْكُرُونَ

O you who have faith! When you stand up for prayer, wash your faces and your hands up to the elbows, and wipe a part of your heads and your feet, up to the ankles. If you are junub, purify yourselves. But if you are sick, or on a journey, or any of you has come from the toilet, or you have touched women, and you cannot find water, then make tayammum with clean ground and wipe a part of your faces and your hands with it. Allah does not desire to put you to hardship, but He desires to purify you, and to complete His blessing upon you so that you may give thanks.

(Al-Ma'idah-6)

وَاذْكُرُوا نِعْمَةَ اللهِ عَلَيْكُمْ وَمِيثَاقَهُ الَّذِى وَاثَقَكُمْ بِهِ إِذْ قُلْتُمْ سَمِعْنَا وَأَطَعْنَا وَاتَّقُوا اللهَ إِنَّ اللهَ عَلِيمٌ بِذَاتِ الصُّدُورِ

Remember Allah's blessing upon you and His covenant with which He has bound you when you said, 'We hear and obey.' And be wary of Allah. Indeed Allah knows best what is in the breasts.

(Al-Ma'idah-7)

وَإِذْ قَالَ مُوسَى لِقَوْمِهِ يَا قَوْمِ اذْكُرُوا نِعْمَةَ اللهِ عَلَيْكُمْ إِذْ جَعَلَ فِيكُمْ أَنْبِيَاءَ وَجَعَلَكُمْ مُلُوكًا وَآتَاكُمْ مَا لَمْ يُؤْتِ أَحَدًا مِنَ الْعَالَمِينَ

When Moses said to his people, 'O my people, remember Allah's blessing upon you when He appointed prophets among you, and made you kings, and gave you what none of the nations were given.

(Al-Ma'idah-20)

هُوَ الَّذِى خَلَقَ لَكُمْ مَا فِى الْأَرْضِ جَمِيعًا ثُمَّ اسْتَوَى إِلَى السَّمَاءِ فَسَوَّاهُنَّ سَبْعَ سَمَاوَاتٍ وَهُوَ بِكُلِّ شَىْءٍ عَلِيمٌ

Cosmic Laws

It is He who created for you all that is in the earth, then He turned to the heaven and fashioned it into seven heavens, and He has knowledge of all things.

(Al-Baqarah-29)

يَا بَنِى إِسْرَائِيلَ اذْكُرُوا نِعْمَتِىَ الَّتِى أَنْعَمْتُ عَلَيْكُمْ وَأَوْفُوا بِعَهْدِى أُوفِ بِعَهْدِكُمْ وَإِيَّايَ فَارْهَبُونِ. يَا بَنِى إِسْرَائِيلَ اذْكُرُوا نِعْمَتِىَ الَّتِى أَنْعَمْتُ عَلَيْكُمْ وَأَنِّى فَضَّلْتُكُمْ عَلَى الْعَالَمِينَ.

O Children of Israel, remember My blessing which I bestowed upon you, and fulfill My covenant that I may fulfill your covenant, and be in awe of Me [alone]. O Children of Israel, remember My blessing which I bestowed upon you, and that I gave you an advantage over all the nations.

(Al-Baqarah 40 and 47)

وَمِنْ حَيْثُ خَرَجْتَ فَوَلِّ وَجْهَكَ شَطْرَ الْمَسْجِدِ الْحَرَامِ وَحَيْثُ مَا كُنْتُمْ فَوَلُّوا وُجُوهَكُمْ شَطْرَهُ لِئَلَّا يَكُونَ لِلنَّاسِ عَلَيْكُمْ حُجَّةٌ إِلَّا الَّذِينَ ظَلَمُوا مِنْهُمْ فَلَا تَخْشَوْهُمْ وَاخْشَوْنِى وَلِأُتِمَّ نِعْمَتِى عَلَيْكُمْ وَلَعَلَّكُمْ تَهْتَدُونَ

And whencesoever you may go out, turn your face towards the Holy Mosque, and wherever you may be, turn your faces towards it, so that the people may have no allegation against you, neither those of them who are wrongdoers. So do not fear them, but fear Me, that I may complete My blessing on you and so that you may be guided.

(Al-Baqarah-150)

يَا أَيُّهَا الَّذِينَ آمَنُوا كُلُوا مِنْ طَيِّبَاتِ مَا رَزَقْنَاكُمْ وَاشْكُرُوا لِلَّهِ إِنْ كُنْتُمْ إِيَّاهُ تَعْبُدُونَ

O you who have faith! Eat of the good things We have provided you, and thank Allah, if it is Him that you worship.

(Al-Baqarah-172)

وَإِذَا طَلَّقْتُمُ النِّسَاءَ فَبَلَغْنَ أَجَلَهُنَّ فَأَمْسِكُوهُنَّ بِمَعْرُوفٍ أَوْ سَرِّحُوهُنَّ بِمَعْرُوفٍ وَلَا تُمْسِكُوهُنَّ ضِرَارًا لِتَعْتَدُوا وَمَنْ يَفْعَلْ ذَلِكَ فَقَدْ ظَلَمَ نَفْسَهُ وَلَا تَتَّخِذُوا آيَاتِ اللَّهِ هُزُوًا وَاذْكُرُوا نِعْمَتَ اللَّهِ عَلَيْكُمْ وَمَا أَنْزَلَ عَلَيْكُمْ مِنَ الْكِتَابِ وَالْحِكْمَةِ يَعِظُكُمْ بِهِ وَاتَّقُوا اللَّهَ وَاعْلَمُوا أَنَّ اللَّهَ بِكُلِّ شَيْءٍ عَلِيمٌ

When you divorce women and they complete their term [of waiting], then either retain them honourably or release them honourably, and do not retain them maliciously in order that you may transgress; and whoever does that certainly wrongs himself. Do not take the signs of Allah in derision, and remember Allah's blessing upon you, and what He has sent down to you of the Book and wisdom, to advise you therewith. Be wary of Allah and know that Allah has knowledge of all things.

(Al-Baqarah-231)

وَإِذْ قُلْنَا ادْخُلُوا هَذِهِ الْقَرْيَةَ فَكُلُوا مِنْهَا حَيْثُ شِئْتُمْ رَغَدًا وَادْخُلُوا الْبَابَ سُجَّدًا وَقُولُوا حِطَّةٌ نَغْفِرْ لَكُمْ خَطَايَاكُمْ وَسَنَزِيدُ الْمُحْسِنِينَ

And when We said, 'Enter this town, and eat thereof freely whencesoever you wish, and enter while prostrating at the gate, and say, "Relieve [us of the burden of our sins]," so that We may forgive your iniquities and We will soon enhance the virtuous.'

(Al-Baqarah-58)

الصَّابِرِينَ وَالصَّادِقِينَ وَالْقَانِتِينَ وَالْمُنْفِقِينَ وَالْمُسْتَغْفِرِينَ بِالْأَسْحَارِ

[They are] patient and truthful, obedient and charitable, and they plead for [Allah's] forgiveness at dawns.

(Al Imran-17)

فَانْقَلَبُوا بِنِعْمَةٍ مِنَ اللَّهِ وَفَضْلٍ لَمْ يَمْسَسْهُمْ سُوءٌ وَاتَّبَعُوا رِضْوَانَ اللَّهِ وَاللَّهُ ذُو فَضْلٍ عَظِيمٍ

So they returned with Allah's blessing and grace, untouched by any harm. They pursued the pleasure of Allah, and Allah is dispenser of a great grace.

(Al Imran-174)

وَمَنْ يُطِعِ اللَّهَ وَالرَّسُولَ فَأُولَٰئِكَ مَعَ الَّذِينَ أَنْعَمَ اللَّهُ عَلَيْهِمْ مِنَ النَّبِيِّينَ وَالصِّدِّيقِينَ وَالشُّهَدَاءِ وَالصَّالِحِينَ ۚ وَحَسُنَ أُولَٰئِكَ رَفِيقًا

Whoever obeys Allah and the Apostle—they are with those whom Allah has blessed, including the prophets and the truthful, the martyrs and the righteous, and excellent companions are they!

(An-Nisa-69)

فَرِحِينَ بِمَا آتَاهُمُ اللَّهُ مِنْ فَضْلِهِ وَيَسْتَبْشِرُونَ بِالَّذِينَ لَمْ يَلْحَقُوا بِهِمْ مِنْ خَلْفِهِمْ أَلَّا خَوْفٌ عَلَيْهِمْ وَلَا هُمْ يَحْزَنُونَ

exulting in what Allah has given them out of His grace, and rejoicing for those who have not yet joined them from [those left] behind them, that they will have no fear, nor will they grieve.

(Al Imran-170)

Who is to blame for our miseries?

We must accept that we are in charge of our own lives and not blame anyone else. As long as we blame others, we will do nothing to make this life better. Jean-Paul Sartre says: If a congenital paralysis does not become a track and field champion, he must be blamed. This is a beautiful view that human should take responsibility for what happens to him. We must never think that when something happens to us, it is the fault of our mother, father, friend, wife, economic status, or society. The idea that we blame someone else allows us to make mistakes again and never make progress. It is like thinking that even when we hit our foot on a rock and we fall down, we hit the rock hard down and say: This rock was guilty that I fell. If you accept that everything outside of us is the result of our thoughts, you will live more easily and are aware that your life is in your hands and you figure it out however you want. If you do not gossip, they will not gossip behind your back. If you do not say bad words, they will not say bad words about you. If you do not have negative thoughts, you will not be attracted to bad things. If you know about the laws of the world, you will experience a beautiful life. My advice is to let go of all external factors and focus on yourself. This is the only way that saves you. You cannot control the whole world not to harm you. However, you can positively think to prevent bad things. You have

Cosmic Laws 147

created all the people and living conditions for yourself. Imagine that you are a professor at a large university. Can you think for one percentage that they call you in a street fight and ask you for help so you pick up a stick or a knife and go to fight? Certainly not. As you never think about fights, you never have a place in street fights. Anyone who pays too much attention to something invites it to their life. What is your focus every day? Do you think of poverty or wealth, do you think of peace or war, do you think of trust or betrayal, do you think of disease or betrayal?

Thus, if your life is not desirable now, it is because of your thoughts and actions in the past. However, by reading this book, you will no longer think like the past and your life will change. You did not gain 30 kilos overnight to lose it overnight. Thus, you need to change your thoughts at the same time to correct them. Do not rush into anything in the world.

The law of evolution

You must know that the law of evolution always helps you. Think about what would happen if everything we thought about appeared suddenly in our lives? As we have both negative and positive thoughts at all times and life would be full of chaos. Everything has an evolutionary trend. For instance, you were first a cell, then two cells, and you multiplied until you became a complete embryo, and when you were born, you grew gradually. This rule works in whatever you can think of. If you plant a seed, what will you have in a few days? A soaked seed. You do not expect it to grow overnight. If you follow the law of evolution in everything, you will not have any stress or haste. In order to have more money, you will not have any problems if you follow this law. For instance, if you have a monthly income of one million tomans, you cannot expect to earn one hundred million tomans next month. You must earn this income gradually. Do not expect your business to boost all at once. You must take the time and develop your business step by step. In addition, you also need time to change your thoughts. Let the positive thoughts come to your mind slowly and let the negative thoughts reduce. Think more positively every day. You will see how much better the world would be for living with this attitude. Use this method if you have things which are difficult for you. For instance, write a page every day to write your book or take ten minutes every day to learn a new language. You will gradually see that all your work has been fulfilled effortlessly.

Spend time for creating a great character. Remember that the greatest empires were not created overnight. A professional athlete does not become a champion overnight.

The law of attraction, vibration, and energy

The law of attraction says that anything you can imagine will happen in the outside world and as you can focus more, it will happen sooner. Every thought that comes to our mind is attracted to the same energy. If you think about poverty, you will become poor, or if you think about wealth, you will become rich ... The world we live in is what we think is solid, and everything is hard and solid, like closets, cars, rocks, etc. If you are aware of quantum science, you will find that bodies are composed of atoms and atoms are composed of tiny particles called strings. These strings are rotating and when the number of their rotations increases, they form a wall which is hard and strong. Consider a fan that you can easily put your hand in when it is turned off, but when it turns on, no one dares to take their fingers in the fan even for testing. As it becomes hard like a wall. This is the most significant thing you need to know about this world. Everything is made of energy and all the things which have the same energy go together without the need to do anything; In other words, each energy is attracted to a similar energy. I give an example so that you understand better. For instance, you put a few kettles of water to boil, what happens when the water boils ... the steam goes into the air without your help ... Now, what if you throw a few stones into the water? It turns out that all of them go under the water. Did you do anything for steam or stone? ... thus, when you think about money, money comes to you. Everything goes towards its own energy. Therefore, all of the things which have the same frequency or vibration will go together. If you know that you are sending vibration at any second, you can easily send the desired vibration by changing your mind. This is the same giant magic lamp I told you about; In other words, think of everything you bring into your life without any efforts. You must learn this law in such a way that it goes to your unconscious mind. For instance, do you remember how you were the first time you drove? You paid attention straight ahead. Sometimes, you had to look at the gear when you wanted to change it and the other things that you know better. However, after a while of training, you drive easily now and even talk on your phone or even if someone asks a question, you answer. It means that driving has reached your unconscious mind. During the early stages, you need a lot of practice. I give you the first key ... Practice ... Practice ... Practice ... Keep it in mind that a lot of wealth does not mean a lot of work. You must be able to change your mind. You have certainly seen the people who work less and earn more money. I will tell you step by step how to do it.

When I worked as a supervisor at the institute, I told the students who complained about studying for eight semesters and had not learned anything, to begin reading from the first semester.
As this way you look at the first lessons with higher awareness and a higher level and then you read and just see that you learn more at this stage, but it seems that nobody likes to come down from their own level but wants to continue the same way because of what people say and after a few years, they leave the institute in despair. I told this example that if you have any information about the law of attraction, leave it aside for a few hours and just read this book without comparing it to anyone or anything. Then, you have to repeat it a few more times as you will understand it correctly after just reading a book a few times and each time you read it, you will find a new point; In other words, you will better understand the subject with a higher level of awareness. This point is one of the golden keys to your learning ... If you read my books, you think a thousand people have read them a thousand times ... A very significant point is that you must accept that you are in charge of your whole life. In this book, you will gradually understand what I mean. Years ago, I asked myself why God blew his spirit into us and what His purpose was. The most beautiful thing I found about this is that we also have the power to create. Believing that human can change his life the way he wants is very exciting and will change your life. In general, the law of attraction states that you have attracted whatever is in your life. This belief gives you power and, more importantly,

you no longer blame anyone but attempt to change your life the way you want. The whole law of attraction is vibration and frequency, both of which have the same meaning. Now, what does vibration mean? ... It means the frequent attention to everything. The law of attraction does not understand "I want" and "I do not want". It will provide you with whatever you order. For instance, imagine that you go to the kitchen to cook and say I want onions, oil, meat and ... you never talk about the things you do not want, for instance you do not say I do not want tomato paste .. I do not want rice ... I do not want potatoes. In fact, you take everything you want and leave whatever you do not need... The law of attraction does not understand "I do not want", it does not work exactly like a copier which copies whatever you give it ... I gave this example to let you know that you must focus only on what you want ... For instance, do not say I do not want this house as it is too small. Think and talk about your dream house. If you are constantly thinking about disease, you will attract more disease, or if you are always thinking about debts and paying bills, you will ask for more debts. Let me tell you something tghat may scare you a bit. If you are a person who is constantly gossiping and talking behind others' back, be aware that all of it will enter your life. If you are constantly reading the accidents section of the newspaper, expect a lot of bad things to happen. If you are constantly complaining about high prices, misery, or poverty, wait for poverty and misery. Those who watch until a street fight or an accident, stand up, take out their phone, and start making videos must wait for similar events in their lives.

Those who constantly talk about betrayal or watch the satellite movies and watch their betrayals and divorces, must wait for divorce and betrayal in theire lives. Describe everything bad that has happened in your life and the same thing will happen to you over and over. Now, you can think a bit and see what the dominant thoughts in your life are and what you often think about and talk to others. Paying attention is not only thinking and talking ... listening is also a kind of attention ... seeing is a kind of paying attention. These are the inputs of your mind. If you keep talking about your miseries, you will bring disaster to your life ... no excuse... think of anything, it will become the same ... If you do not resist accepting that you can build your life with your thoughts, your will will change. Belief that the world is full of abundance will save you and that this is exactly God's justice. If you think about something more, you will receive more of it. Hold your thoughts in your hands so that your life is in your hands. It does not matter what your current conditions are, begin building your life now. You may ask how and when we acheive what we want. I have to say that only God knows the times. As you send more vibrations, you make this time shorter. Imagine that you throw a stone into the water. It creates small waves which get bigger the farther away from the center. We must live our lives on such orbits. Nobody can go from the first orbit to the last one.

For instance, a person who earns one million Tomans a month cannot reach a hundred million Tomans overnight or a person who has a bad emotional relationship cannot correct his feelings overnight ... Understanding this issue will save you from despair in this path and also prevents you from being impatient. Little by little, you get what you want.

Life-giving sentences

The sentences which you have to read over and over to penetrate deep into your soul and gain a deep understanding of it. Remember that you must not have a lot of information, you must act on it.

1. Do not wait for the opportunity, create it
2. Do not retreat, pass
3. Do not compare, be unique
4. Do not run away from life, accept it.
5. Be simple, then you will be full of mystery.
6. Do not judge, act fairly.
7. Be yourself to become unique.
8. Be a servant of God, then you will be free from any bully.
9. Do not close your eyes to reality, open your mind
10. Accept your weakness: You will become strong.
11. Love to become popular
12. Remain silent to become aware
13. Leave interference to seek for guidance
14. Speak less to be effective
15. Rule yourself to rule the universe
16. Be aware of the darkness in mind to lighten the lives.
17. Even if you are in good conditions today, practice for a better day.
18. Be honest with yourself and do not worry about what people say about you
19. Do not want to attract others just for beauty and charm
20. Whenever you are tempted to make sarcastic remarks on people, remember that the acid burns its own side.

21. Rude words destroy friendships but kindness connects everyone to each other
22. Always help others to reach excellence.
23. Be like God in love. Love unexpectedly.
24. Be smart for understanding and smarter for acting.
25. Be appreciative and express gratitude.
26. Get rid of jealousy and hatred as it burns you first.
27. Strengthen contentment in your being and be grateful for having real friends.
28. Do not try to keep others satisfied with yourself.
29. While talking to others, let them speak.
30. Ignore the fears and beliefs of others about disease and get rid of negative thoughts.
31. Try to your spirit high and do not care about external conditions.
32. Consider happiness as your daily routine.
33. Stand in the mirror and compliment on yourself.
34. Start giving away from your home and give to others as much as you can.
35. Repeat and repeat the daily emphatic phrases.
36. Have faith that God is the only source of goodness.
37. If you suffer from a disease, stop talking and thinking about it and stop complaining.
38. Ignore the toxic words of others
39. Do not forget to trust in God and ask Him for help every day.
40. Set time for thanksgiving each day
41. Watch motivational movies and read the biographies of successful people.
42. Dedicate time on meditation every day

43. Look for happy subjects, otherwise sorrow will find you
44. Be more the source of action than reaction. Emotional reactions cover the facts like a cloud.
45. If you want to get over those who misbehaved you, tell good things about them.
46. Do not pay attention if others criticize you weather right or wrong but be grateful to them from the bottom of your heart.
47. Know that serving people will make you happy and you will never enjoy anything like it.
48. You show your weakness and humiliation by humiliating others. Always respect people.
49. Even a whirlwind of sorrow disappears with jokes and laughter. Calm down and believe that everything will end in your favor soon.

You do not know how beautiful life is:

When you get what you want miraculously. When you feel that you have a positive effect on the world around you. When your body is healthy. When you can travel wherever you want. Every time you talk to God, tears appear in your eyes and you want to hug Him lovingly, kiss Him and say: Thank you so much for everything. When thousands of people pray good things for you every day. When more wealth-creating ideas come to your mind every day. When you can realize the promises you made to your mother in the past and prepare a beautiful life for her. When you find lots of friends around the world. When you can buy anything you want and you never are not worried about the price. When you go anywhere in the world, it is as if the best people in the world are there. When the world shows you more surprises every day. When the world gives you more awareness every day. When you see people laughing and I tell myself that it was really worth it staying and practicing and also raising my awareness every day. It is worth studying every day.

It is worth listening to my professors. It is worth accepting that I had to raise my level of awareness every day; I thank God for having mercy on me. I am learning every day as I know this is the only path to happiness.

Law of abandonment

In the Quran, the Prophet is repeatedly told: do not pay attention to what you do not want but pay attention to God and what you want. God even instructs the Prophet not to pay attention to those who mock the Quran since if someone pays attention to the unwanted, they absorb the same things.

See how God talks about abandonment in the verses below.

اتَّبِعْ مَا أُوحِيَ إِلَيْكَ مِنْ رَبِّكَ لَا إِلَهَ إِلَّا هُوَ وَأَعْرِضْ عَنِ الْمُشْرِكِينَ

Follow that which has been revealed to you from your Lord, there is no god except Him, and turn away from the polytheists.
(Al-An'am-106)

خُذِ الْعَفْوَ وَأْمُرْ بِالْعُرْفِ وَأَعْرِضْ عَنِ الْجَاهِلِينَ

Adopt [a policy of] excusing [the faults of people], bid what is right, and turn away from the ignorant.
(Al-A'raf-199)

Cosmic Laws

سَيَحْلِفُونَ بِاللّهِ لَكُمْ إِذَا انْقَلَبْتُمْ إِلَيْهِمْ لِتُعْرِضُوا عَنْهُمْ فَأَعْرِضُوا عَنْهُمْ إِنَّهُمْ رِجْسٌ وَمَأْوَاهُمْ جَهَنَّمُ جَزَاءً بِمَا كَانُوا يَكْسِبُونَ

They will swear to you by Allah when you return to them, that you may leave them alone. So leave them alone. They are indeed filth, and their refuge shall be hell, a requital for what they used to earn.
(At-Tawbah-95)

وَإِذَا رَأَيْتَ الَّذِينَ يَخُوضُونَ فِى آيَاتِنَا فَأَعْرِضْ عَنْهُمْ حَتَّى يَخُوضُوا فِى حَدِيثٍ غَيْرِهِ وَإِمَّا يُنْسِيَنَّكَ الشَّيْطَانُ فَلَا تَقْعُدْ بَعْدَ الذِّكْرَى مَعَ الْقَوْمِ الظَّالِمِينَ

When you see those who gossip impiously about Our signs, avoid them until they engage in some other discourse; but if Satan makes you forget, then, after remembering, do not sit with the wrongdoing lot.
(Al-An'am-68)

وَيَقُولُونَ طَاعَةٌ فَإِذَا بَرَزُوا مِنْ عِنْدِكَ بَيَّتَ طَائِفَةٌ مِنْهُمْ غَيْرَ الَّذِى تَقُولُ وَاللّهُ يَكْتُبُ مَا يُبَيِّتُونَ فَأَعْرِضْ عَنْهُمْ وَتَوَكَّلْ عَلَى اللّهِ وَكَفَى بِاللّهِ وَكِيلًا

hey profess obedience [to you], but when they go out from your presence, a group of them conspire overnight [to do] something other than what you say. But Allah records what they conspire overnight. So disregard them and put your trust in Allah, for Allah suffices as trustee.
(An-Nisa-81)

فَاصْدَعْ بِمَا تُؤْمَرُ وَأَعْرِضْ عَنِ الْمُشْرِكِينَ

So proclaim what you have been commanded, and turn away from the polytheists.
(Al Hejr-94)

قَدْ أَفْلَحَ الْمُؤْمِنُونَ

Certainly, the faithful have attained salvation
(Al-Mu'minun-1)

الَّذِينَ هُمْ فِى صَلَاتِهِمْ خَاشِعُونَ

those who are humble in their prayers,
(Al-Mu'minun-2)

$$وَالَّذِينَ هُمْ عَنِ اللَّغْوِ مُعْرِضُونَ$$

avoid vain talk,
(Al-Mu'minun-3)

$$وَإِذَا سَمِعُوا اللَّغْوَ أَعْرَضُوا عَنْهُ وَقَالُوا لَنَا أَعْمَالُنَا وَلَكُمْ أَعْمَالُكُمْ سَلَامٌ عَلَيْكُمْ لَا نَبْتَغِي الْجَاهِلِينَ$$

and when they hear vain talk, they avoid it and say, 'Our deeds belong to us, and your deeds belong to you. Peace be to you. We do not court the ignorant.'
(Al-Qasas-55)

$$فَأَعْرِضْ عَنْهُمْ وَانْتَظِرْ إِنَّهُمْ مُنْتَظِرُونَ$$

So turn away from them, and wait. They too are waiting.
(As-Sajdah-30)

$$فَأَعْرِضْ عَنْ مَنْ تَوَلَّى عَنْ ذِكْرِنَا وَلَمْ يُرِدْ إِلَّا الْحَيَاةَ الدُّنْيَا$$

So avoid those who turn away from Our remembrance and desire nothing but the life of the world.
(An-Najm-29)

$$أُولَئِكَ الَّذِينَ يَعْلَمُ اللَّهُ مَا فِي قُلُوبِهِمْ فَأَعْرِضْ عَنْهُمْ وَعِظْهُمْ وَقُلْ لَهُمْ فِي أَنْفُسِهِمْ قَوْلًا بَلِيغًا$$

They are the ones whom Allah knows as to what is in their hearts. So let them alone, and advise them, and speak to them concerning themselves far-reaching words.
(An-Nisa-63)

Make the best use of this law in life. If you are upset about something, ignore it. If you pay attention to anything, you invite it into your life. If you want someone to go out of your life, do not fight them. Just do not pay attention to them to go out of your life.

What is your mission?

I must say that God is very fair. He has set the laws in this world which have nothing to do with your past or your future. He only deals with the moment right now. You become your dominant frequencies and thoughts. God has let you decide your own destiny and this is God's justice. God never judges your capabilities. He created you infinitely. He has given you the authority to develop your talents The authority is with you to find and carry out the mission of your life. Every particle in the world is looking for a mission and is being led to its set place while moving in its orbit. This is the mission of the universe. In Surah Ya-Sin verse 38, God says: The sun runs on to its place of rest: That is the ordaining of the All-mighty, the All-knowing. As for the moon, we have ordained its phases, until it becomes like an old palm leaf. Neither it behooves the sun to overtake the moon, nor may the night outrun the day, and each swims in an orbit.

Thus, aimlessness and lack of mission have no meaning at all in this lawful and orderly world. Every little disorder is doomed. The slightest aimlessness is doomed to destruction. Our mission becomes clear and comes to power and grows bigger at every moment. If we get in line with the laws of the world, we will be empowered and guided. If we are not in line with the world, we will stop where we are and it means falling behind and not growing. You must be able to succeed through contradictions. We were born to grow in all dimensions by knowing ourselves and facing different experiences. Facing these challenges and solving them enhance our ability of problem-solving. Growing depends on solving problems.

Our mission is not just to do routine things. Instead, we discover our interests and move on to try the unknown and

face the new challenges we call experience. You will have no experience unless you act according what you know. You certainly ask yourself these questions every day
- I do not know what my mission is? How do I find the mission of my life?
- If the mission is so important, why do I not have any enthusiasm to find it?
- How can I reach my true love and success?
- Why am I scared to start? What if I do not succeed?
- How can I find my main goal and mission and enjoy doing it and also become rich?

One of your most significant and enjoyable tasks is to find your mission. Your mission is something that you can do with love and the passage of time is not essential to you. If you are doing the same thing all day, do not feel the passage of time. The same thing you do again even if you are not paid. Something that does not make you tired. You do it eagerly and you still want to do it over and over. Doing the thing that makes your eyes sparkle and put a smile on your face. You will fall in love with yourself and admire yourself.

Mission is what you feel you were born for doing that. Mission is doing something that makes you feel closer to God and makes you proud of yourself by doing so. The first step to understand mission is to know that God guides everything. The world is based on guidance. Everyone is guided when they are in line with the laws of the world. Just as a seed is led towards growth and light as it is exposed to the right soil, water, and light, and to become a tree and bear fruit, we are also guided as we decide to move and gain more experience. The second step is to enter the unknown parts of your life and enhance the scope of your experiences. You must increase your knowledge and awareness every day. It is never as: Sit in a corner and find your mission by thinking and visualizing. Instead, as you walk, you will face the problems which will help you gain experience and be more clear about yourself and find your interest. The third step is to understand that if you serve the universe, expand the world, and create value, the world will also expand you. Our mission is to know ourselves at every moment. Our mission is to grow and receive guidance and inspiration which comes to us at every moment in the form of specific signs. Our mission is to recognize these symptoms and take them seriously to be guided step by step. Why? since we have been created infinitely. The superior mission of our lives is a great vision. A very sacred, perfect and extraordinary purpose as we cannot stop growing, we cannot stop expanding the world. We cannot stop being useful to the universe. We cannot make excuses and limit ourselves to one thing and stop studying. It is enough to break the boundaries of beliefs and enter a new field of experience. Our life experiences may be cooking a new food, sewing a new dress, drawing, practicing shooting a ball in a certain way, losing weight, experiencing a new job, making a small change in business, having a short trip, reading a new book, learning a new language, moving to another city, or your mission may be not doing something or changing attitudes. Perhaps quitting a job, quitting a relationship, quitting addiction, quitting resentment and hatred, quitting bad language or quitting bad habits that can we be led to the next step only by quitting them. If you do not take these steps, you will fall behind every day and face bigger contradictions and suddenly you will not be able to solve problems and have to give up.

This is God's justice when you decide to change, you can quickly see the external changes. God sends His hands for helping you. Perhaps one of these changes is getting familiar with a teacher. God speaks to you through him.

Self-confidence and self-esteem

Self-confidence means the ability to do things and self-esteem means feeling valued. Self-confidence means the ability to fulfill things. The more skills you learn, the more confident you become. By fulfilling new things and gaining more experiences, your self-confidence will increase gradually and your fears will disappear. Learning a new language will help you. Remember that the more skillfully you fulfill a task, the more confident you will be. Thus, focus on learning a job to gain a skill or expertise. Indeed, self-esteem is the amount of value that everyone person places on themselves. The sense of being valued is gained through beliefs, experiences, feelings, emotions, etc. Thus, the person sees himself worthy and capable;

Thus, if you have negative thoughts about yourself, you have low self-esteem. If you have a good and positive feeling about yourself, you have high self-esteem. Here are some signs of self-esteem.
- Love ourselves and accept that everyone in this world is valuable
- Take responsibility of our own lives.
- Love to learn and gain new experiences and feel effective.
- Deal with challenges and problems appropriately.

People's self-esteem and self-confidence go back to childhood, being formed and created by parents and others. Stand in front of the mirror for a few minutes every day and compliment on yourself. If you love yourself, the whole world will love you, while if you do not love yourself, the world will prove to you that you are not lovable. Never put your self-esteem in someone who does not want you. Never beg anyone to love you. Never beg for love. If you do not have sufficient self-confidence and self-esteem, you need to learn it again. Visit our website and prepare the course on self-confidence and self-esteem and listen to it. Self-confidence and self-esteem are two wings for your flight. You cannot do anything without them.

To increase self-esteem, you can:
- Create positive relationships.
- Learn to say no
- Challenge yourself.
- Accept unpleasant events.
- Set your goals.
- Consult with effective people.
- Overcome bad temptations.
- Be kind to yourself.
- Value yourself
- Behave respectfully.
- Speak thoughtfully.
- Study.
- Eat the best foods.
- Regard yourself worthy of the best.
- Go to the best restaurants.
- Do not talk to bad people.
- Wear nice clothes.
- Be polite and respectful.
- Consider yourself valuable.
- Go everywhere you are invited with awareness.

Belief in abundance

We are not supposed to always have problems in our lives. We are not supposed to fail at achieving our dreams or helping someone. Shortage is not our final destiny. You have been created to live in abundance. However, if you get yourself into trouble, the belief in shortage will be formed in you. As long as you think of shortage, you will never achieve excessive wealth. You must destroy this belief in shortage and create the belief in abundance. God can bring abundance to your life in the ways you can never imagine. If you trust God, He will give you something beyond your income and salary, as well as beyond anything you have ever seen. You do not know what God has set aside for you.

You are not aware of the progress, opportunities, and divine kindness that He has set to be in the path of your life. God gets happy to bless you. God owns everything and can guide you to your goals. Strengthen the belief in abundance in yourself. Look around every day and create a belief in abundance. For instance, look around and see how many clothing stores are in your neighborhood and then imagine how many clothing stores are in your country and how many clothing stores are in the world. It cannot be counted at all. Now, see how many pairs of shoes are in the world. How many cars are around the world? How many humans are in the world? Who knows how many leaves are on the trees of the world. How many dots are in the words written in the books. How many pebbles are in the deserts? Look around and find more examples of abundance in the world every day. It has been always said that natural resources such as water, electricity and gas are running out, and now the world produces electricity from solar energy. It cannot be over. The world is always expanding and growing. Considering many years ago, you would see that even the ways of earning money have increased. The mass media has increased. There is more of anything you can think. There are endless home appliances to amenities and money and everything you can imagine. The world is expanding day by day and you must keep telling yourself about this expansion. The God who has created this world has thought of everything. However, this does not mean to waste, but the appropriate use of blessings is a form of thanksgiving. Find new blessings every day and be grateful. Life becomes very enjoyable for you. Belief in shortage always puts pressure on you and draws fears in your heart. It makes you afraid of spending money and you make life difficult for those around you. You have come to enjoy this world. God provides us with sustenance and there is no lack in His throne. He is highly generous. Do not ask for less. If your wishes are not big enough to scare you, then you have no wish at all.

Last word
Congratulations if you fully read this book as I know that your desire to achieve your desires is very high now. Most people cannot even read a book to the end. Please read this book several times and prepare the audio file from our website and listen to some part of it every day to penetrate into your unconscious mind. Your car is your mobile class. It is the best situation to listen to audio files. In order to raise your awareness of wealth and emotional relationships, as well as self-confidence and self-esteem and how to improve life skills whether at work or marriage, we have prepared some unique audio and video courses which are available on the website. Visit the website and prepare any of our courses that you need. Read and listen to this book and our files for a year and

practice them every day. Then, you will clearly see the changes later.

Share your opinions with your friends on our website and know about their results, and if they want guidance, share your experiences with them.

I wish happiness, health, and wealth to all my friends wherever you are in the world.

Farewell

Our website: www.moghadasii.com

This book is translated to 4 languages

Kidsocado Publishing House
Vancouver, Canada

Phone : +1 (833) 633 8654
WhatsApp: +1 (236) 333 7248
Email: info@kidsocado.com
https://kidsocadopublishinghouse.com
https://kphclub.com

www.ingramcontent.com/pod-product-compliance
Lightning Source LLC
Chambersburg PA
CBHW071417070526
44578CB00003B/589